BLOCKCHAIN
FOR
EVERYONE

BLOCKCHAIN FOR EVERYONE

How I Learned the Secrets of the New Millionaire Class (And You Can, Too)

SIR JOHN HARGRAVE

GALLERY BOOKS

New York   London   Toronto   Sydney   New Delhi

G

Gallery Books
An Imprint of Simon & Schuster, Inc.
1230 Avenue of the Americas
New York, NY 10020

Copyright © 2019 by Sir John Hargrave

This publication contains the opinions and ideas of its author. It is sold with the understanding that neither the author nor the publisher is engaged in rendering legal, tax, investment, insurance, financial, accounting, or other professional advice or services. If the reader requires such advice or services, a competent professional should be consulted. Relevant laws vary from state to state. The strategies outlined in this book may not be suitable for every individual, and are not guaranteed or warranted to produce any particular results.

No warranty is made with respect to the accuracy or completeness of the information contained herein, and both the author and the publisher specifically disclaim any responsibility for any liability, loss or risk, personal or otherwise, which is incurred as a consequence, directly or indirectly, of the use and application of any of the contents of this book.

Certain names and identifying details have been changed, some events have been reordered or combined and some characters are composites.

All rights reserved, including the right to reproduce this book or portions thereof in any form whatsoever. For information, address Gallery Books Subsidiary Rights Department, 1230 Avenue of the Americas, New York, NY 10020.

First Gallery Books hardcover edition August 2019

GALLERY BOOKS and colophon are registered trademarks of Simon & Schuster, Inc.

For information about special discounts for bulk purchases, please contact Simon & Schuster Special Sales at 1-866-506-1949 or business@simonandschuster.com.

The Simon & Schuster Speakers Bureau can bring authors to your live event. For more information or to book an event, contact the Simon & Schuster Speakers Bureau at 1-866-248-3049 or visit our website at www.simonspeakers.com.

Interior design by Davina Mock-Maniscalco

Manufactured in the United States of America

10   9   8   7   6   5   4   3   2   1

Library of Congress Cataloging-in-Publication Data is available.

ISBN 978-1-9821-1354-4
ISBN 978-1-9821-1376-6 (ebook)

CONTENTS

BLOCKCHAIN FOR EVERYONE

PREFACE

When I bought bitcoin in 2013, the price was $125. Four years later, that same bitcoin was worth $20,000—a staggering *15,900 percent gain*.

Swept up in the excitement, plenty of investors bought that same bitcoin at $20,000. A year later, the price had plummeted to $3,500—an equally staggering *83 percent loss*.

Like the gold rush of the 1850s and the dot-com boom of the 1990s, investors in this world of "new money" are mining massive wealth, seemingly overnight. Great fortunes are built before breakfast, then lost along with lunch.

How can an ordinary investor build a fortune, without betting the farm?

Like you, I'm an ordinary investor. And I did bet the farm.

That's the hilarious, harrowing story I'm about to tell you. I won big, then lost big, then . . . well, you'll see. It's an adrenaline-fueled roller-coaster ride, full of colorful characters straight out of central casting—a strangely addictive story you'll want to read cover to cover. Maybe in a single sitting!

Along the way, you'll learn about bitcoin, the underlying technology called blockchain, and a strategy for making responsible investing decisions with this new money: how to build a fortune without betting the farm.

I'm an ordinary investor, not a financial adviser, so it's important to read the entire story—both the stomach-churning risks and the money-earning rewards—before you make your own decisions. Do your homework. Think for yourself. And never invest more than you are willing to lose.

I was willing to lose a lot—and I did. But I gained something priceless: the knowledge I'm about to share with you. Use it well.

Health, wealth, and happiness,
Sir John Hargrave

PART 1

THE BEGINNING

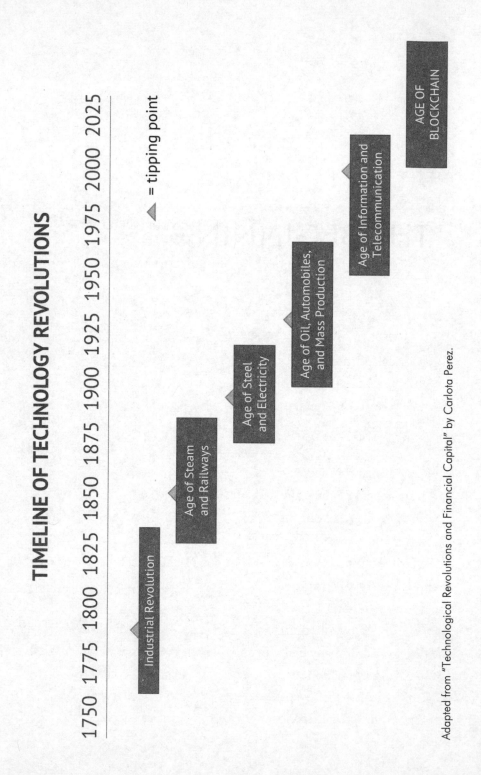

TIMELINE OF TECHNOLOGY REVOLUTIONS

1750 1775 1800 1825 1850 1875 1900 1925 1950 1975 2000 2025

▲ = tipping point

Industrial Revolution

Age of Steam and Railways

Age of Steel and Electricity

Age of Oil, Automobiles, and Mass Production

Age of Information and Telecommunication

AGE OF BLOCKCHAIN

Adapted from "Technological Revolutions and Financial Capital" by Carlota Perez.

CHAPTER 1

How I Became a Dot-com Millionaire

"I got you a surprise."

The year was 1995, and my wife, Jade, and I were standing outside the technology media company where I worked. A black stretch limo, sleek as a hot buttered dolphin, rounded the corner and drove up to us.

I laughed and squeezed her hand. "This is the best birthday ever."

"It gets better," she promised.

Sticking his head out the sunroof, my coworker Ned yelled, "Wooo! Happy thirtieth birthday!"

The limousine doors opened, and out spilled a raucous group of friends and coworkers, young technology professionals riding high on the dot-com bubble.

"This is really something else," I observed as Jade and I climbed into the limo. Our company had recently gone public on the New York Stock Exchange, and everyone was celebrating: party hats, champagne . . . There was a platter of oysters perched precariously on a seat, and when my friend and coworker Genevieve climbed in, she accidentally sat on them.

"Gen sat on the oysters!" Chris shouted, and everyone erupted in howls, including Gen.

"Have some shrimp!" Chris shouted, throwing a shrimp at me. "And a boilermaker!" He handed me a drink.

"What's a boilermaker?" I asked.

"Beer with a shot of whiskey!" Chris responded cheerfully. "Boilermakers for everyone!" He stuck his head out the sunroof as the limo pulled out. "Boilermakers for Boston!" He grabbed a handful of shrimp and tossed them at an innocent pedestrian. The limo erupted in laughter.

"A drive-by shrimping!" Gen laughed.

"This will end badly," I predicted, taking a big swig. It tasted like jet fuel and hops. "Where are we going?"

"That's the best part." Jade's eyes sparkled. "You know how you've always wanted to see that comedy hypnotist?"

"Get out," I said. "The one who gets you onstage and makes you think you're a donkey?"

"That's the one."

"You are the most thoughtful wife ever." I squeezed her thigh.

"Hey, what's our stock price?" Ned asked.

"Closed just above $19," Gen replied, dabbing at the cocktail sauce on her dress with a handful of napkins.

There was a brief silence as everyone calculated the value of their stock options while pretending not to. I did some quick mental math and had one of the greatest shocks of my life.

I was a millionaire.

True, it was just on paper; I didn't have a million dollars in cash. I had stock options worth a million dollars. That meant if I stayed with the company another year *and* the stock price stayed at $19, I could then sell the stock, making a million dollars in the trade.

Who cared? Technically, I was a millionaire. On my thirtieth birthday!

No one knew how many stock options everyone else held, so we had to keep all this to ourselves. Suddenly a dam exploded, and the limo erupted in cheers. "Woo-hoo!" yelled Chris, lighting up a Roman candle and firing it out the sunroof. *FOOM.*

"What are you doing?!" Genevieve laughed. *FOOM.*

"Hey!" The limo driver pounded on the glass partition. "You have to stop that." *FOOM.*

I looked over at Jade. I knew she had already made the same calculations, probably figuring in tax and depreciation. She had also mentally run several what-if scenarios with best-case, worst-case, and likely-case stock prices in a year, when we could cash out. We shared a kiss.

"Get a limo, you two!" Chris shouted now, then stuck his head out the window. "Limos for everyone!"

Maybe it was the boilermaker kicking in, but the scene suddenly seemed surreal. I had grown up in a middle-class neighborhood in Ohio, then moved to Boston to become a comedy writer. I wasn't born into wealth or privilege; my trust fund was a Honda Civic. Now I was a millionaire riding in a limo?

Head spinning, I tried to reverse engineer how this had happened.

- ✦ True, I had **worked like crazy** since graduating college five years earlier. But this seemed *too* good, like something you'd see in the opening chapter of a book. I looked around, wondering if we were already at the comedy hypnotist and I was dreaming the entire scene.

- ✦ When the Internet happened, it was **the right place and the right time**. I had landed a job with a media company that published computer magazines like *PC Magazine* and *Computer Shopper*. (For younger readers, magazines were stacks of colored paper that were sold in things called bookstores.)

- **We understood this stuff.** The company was one of the first to start publishing its articles online, so we were well-positioned when Internet companies started taking over Wall Street. We were not only reporting on dot-coms; we had also built one of the biggest dot-coms. We were dot-com double dipping.

- I was also **following my passion**: the Internet was so intellectually fascinating, so technologically seductive, that I couldn't stop playing with it. I wanted to share it. So I fused my comedy writing with my love of technology to become a comedy-tech writer, explaining the Internet in a way that was simple and fun.

- Finally, there was an element of **luck**—but not as much as you might think. (See the chart below.)

How to Become an Internet Millionaire

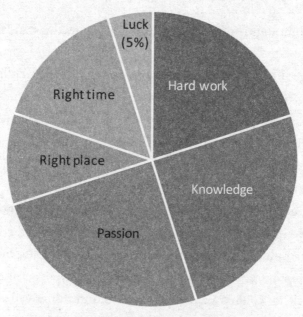

95 percent of this you can learn in this book.

"My friends," I said, raising my half-drained boilermaker, "it is a privilege to share my thirtieth birthday with you, the people I love so much, doing the job I love so much, with the wife"—I looked at Jade, her eyes shining—"with the wife I love so much. A toast to health, wealth, and happiness."

"Hear, hear!" shouted everyone in the limousine, and someone cranked up Madonna's "Ray of Light."

"Of all the decisions I've made," I whispered to Jade, "the best one was marrying you." I drained my boilermaker and leaned back with my arm around the love of my life. Nerds were cool, the Internet was hot, and new media was the new black. *Surely*, I thought, *this is the greatest time to be alive.*

The comedy hypnotist wasn't that funny and he didn't hypnotize me. He did bring me up onstage as one of several volunteers, but then I tried to steal the microphone from him so I could hypnotize the audience myself.

"You are all getting sleepy!" I slurred as the hypnotist tried to wrestle control of the mic. I grabbed it from him, and he chased me as I weaved my way through the other volunteers, who legitimately thought they were donkeys. "Hee-haw," I said, lightly touching each one on the head as I ran by. "Hee-haw. Hee-haw."

A bouncer jumped onto the stage and pulled me down, and I landed on the opening band's drum kit. A cymbal crashed on my head.

"On behalf of the boilermakers," Chris whispered to Jade, who had her head buried in her hands, "I'd like to apologize."

A few months later, and reminiscent of that cymbal, the entire stock market came crashing down. The dot-com bubble burst, taking the world economy with it. Jade and I went from being millionaires back to being thousandaires. Eventually we lost all our money.

Then we got it all back again, with a new technology called **blockchain**.

This book is the story of that journey from riches to rags to riches again. I'm sharing it with you because I want you to become rich while hopefully avoiding the rags. Wealth is not a zero-sum game. There is limitless abundance for all, enough for everyone on earth—and blockchain will help us share that wealth.

You don't need any special powers to understand blockchain. All you need is a *love of learning*. This you already have: it's why you're reading this story! So be a learning sponge, soak up knowledge, and quench your thirst.

I thought the dot-com days were the greatest time to be alive. I never thought I'd be lucky enough to see that kind of excitement and energy a second time. If anything, blockchain is even better.

Here's the story of how I ended up on the front line of the Blockchain Revolution.

CHAPTER 2

Meeting with the Master

The thing I remember most about Martin's home office was the fish tank.

It wasn't the rich mahogany desk, the bowl of imported Chinese candies, the bookshelves cluttered with photos of Martin posing with various tech CEOs. It was that amazing fish tank, which looked like it was airlifted out of SeaWorld.

"Martin, you'd give the New England Aquarium a run for its money," I said, admiring the coral reefs teeming with angelfish. I was simultaneously captivated by Martin's fish and by the reflection of Martin's frizzy hair. It was a high-humidity day.

He chuckled. "The only secret to owning an aquarium like this is to *have a good fish guy.*" He punctuated each word with a jab of his finger. "The fish guy does all the work. I just enjoy it."

Of course Martin had a fish guy. His first career was as a successful tech executive, the guy they'd bring in to turn around troubled companies. Then he "retired" into a second career as an entrepreneurial adviser and early-stage investor. In the Boston startup scene, all roads ran through Martin.

"Down to business." Martin motioned to the two leather chairs, and we sat down. He was dressed in the traditional tech investor uniform—Patagonia vest and jeans—but that frizz! I guess his hair was his trademark: mildly eccentric millionaire. Good branding.

I pulled out my laptop and loaded up a PowerPoint slide. "The good news is, our company, Media Shower, is wrapping up the year with 25 percent growth over last year."

"Okay. Just 25 percent?"

"Well, that's also the bad news."

He paused.

"*Hockey stick growth*," he said. "Investors want to see up and to the right."

"Remember that we've built this business ourselves. Sweat equity and savings. Jade and I work our asses off. Sixty-hour weeks. Five years? Ten years? I've lost track."

"And how big are we?"

"Two million in annual revenue."

"Not bad for a mom-and-pop business." I winced as he said that. "And how big do we want to grow?"

"A billion dollars."

"Right. So again"—Martin put his hand up at a forty-five-degree angle—"hockey stick."

"Check this out." I pulled out my Moleskine notebook and opened it up.

"That's my daily affirmation." I flipped through page after page. "That's my mind hack."

"Well, you're 0.2 percent of the way there."

"It's what a billion dollars *represents*. I want this company to make a dent in the universe."

"You want to be the next Steve Jobs."

"Well, the position did recently open up."

I am running a billion dollar company

I am running a billion dollar company

I am running a billion dollar company

I am running a billion dollar company

I am running n billion dollar company

I am running a billion dollar company

I am running a billion dollar company

I am running a billion dollar company

I am running a billion dollar company

I am running a billion dollar company

I am running a billion dollar company

I am running a billion dollar company

I am running a billion dollar company

I am running a billion dollar company

I am running a billion dollar company

I am running a billion dollar company

I am running a billion dollar company

"Okay." Martin took all this calmly. "Let me try to trace the path. You started out doing comedy, right?"

"I'm sorry it wasn't Harvard," I said. "But I did go back for my MBA."

"That was before or after you were fired?"

"Which time?"

"There was more than one firing?"

I shrugged. "Some people were born to be leaders, not followers."

"So from comedy to MBA, and now you've built this little Internet agency." The word "little" was a Brillo pad on an open ego. "How many clients now?"

"Our agency," I bristled, "has over a hundred clients. A dozen full-time employees. A hundred freelancers."

"All right. Well, technology investors are looking for the next Facebook. They want a unicorn."

"What's a unicorn?" It was the first time I had heard the term outside of a fairy tale.

"A billion-dollar company."

"Unicorns aren't real," I pointed out.

Martin reached for an imported candy and unwrapped it thoughtfully. He popped it in his mouth.

"Unicorns are a myth," I added, pressing the point.

"I'm thinking how we get you from two million to a billion. You've pivoted so many times."

"You know who else pivots?" I shot back. "Nature. Constantly trying new things. Only we call it 'evolution.'"

Martin raised his eyebrows and tilted his head as if thinking, *Point taken.* "There's nothing wrong with this path you're on. But if you really want to take it to the next level, you've got to evolve faster. How many Internet agencies are there?"

"I don't know. Infinity." I threw up my hands. "It's cutthroat."

"That's because all agencies are the same. You're all selling salt. Might come in a fancier box, but it's still salt." These words stung, but this was why I was paying him.

The fish tank hummed as Martin sucked on his candy. The afternoon sunlight caught his hair in a kind of frizzy halo.

"If you want to build wealth," he said, "you've got to zig when everyone else is zagging."

"Zag when everyone else is zigging," I recited automatically.

"Good. Now, there's got to be something in your business that holds special promise."

"We've been down this road, Martin."

"Then what's intellectually interesting to you? Sometimes you can follow your passion."

"Blockchain," I blurted out.

"What's blockchain?"

"You've heard of bitcoin?" I asked.

"Sure. It's like electronic money. They use it to buy drugs on the dark web."

"Really, Martin? One of the greatest technological achievements of our time, and you reduce it to drug money? It is so much more than that." I opened my Moleskine notebook again and sketched out:

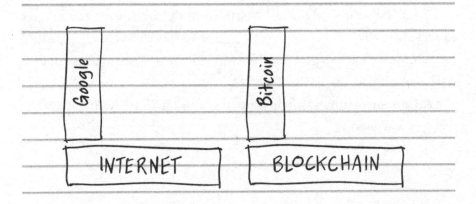

"Here's the Internet," I explained. "Think of the Internet as a platform upon which we build websites like Google. But how does the Internet actually *work*? I've been working on the Internet my entire life, and I still think it's powered by hamsters."

"You don't need to know how an engine works to drive a car."

"Right." I pointed at him. "Now think of blockchain as a platform, like the Internet. It's the underlying technology behind bitcoin, and I think it's going to be huge."

"Why?"

"Have you seen the price of bitcoin lately?"

My adviser shook his head.

"It's over $100, Martin! There are people who bought bitcoin when it was a dollar. Imagine buying $10,000 worth of bitcoin a couple of years ago. That would be worth $10 million today!"

"One million," Martin corrected me.

My face turned red. "Point is," I stammered, "there's something here. We picked up a huge new banking client and they're having us write a whole series about blockchain." I told him the name of the banking client.

He whistled. "That's a feather in your cap."

"This is a big opportunity, Martin. I am ready to go big or go home."

"Well, let's hope we go big." Martin smiled. "I'd hate for you to have to go home."

"But if we have to go home"—I smiled back—"isn't that partially a reflection on you, my adviser?"

An automatic timer switched off, and the aquarium went dark. That fish guy was good.

CHAPTER 3

The Epic Origin Story

"Would you look at that. Humans still work here."

Jade and I were seated in the lobby of our local bank, watching a couple of glassy-eyed tellers manage the line of lunchtime customers like a snake slowly digesting field mice. I had opened an account here in college; ten bank mergers later, they held our personal and business accounts, home mortgage, and line of credit.

"Yes," my wife responded sweetly, "and I stand in that line each week to talk to the humans."

"And I appreciate it. That would drive me crazy."

"Some of us have to deposit the checks from our clients," she replied, checking her phone, "so others can go wining and dining our clients."

"Just dining," I corrected her. "Haven't done any wining in eight years."

"You were *whining* just this morning. About not having time to meditate."

"Meditation is the reason I haven't been wining."

"The kids need an early pickup today," she said, looking at her screen.

"I don't even enjoy the dining," I confessed. "It feels so phony. *Pay us a lot of money and we'll take you out to a nice dinner*. Why don't we charge them less, they take themselves out to dinner, and we eliminate the middleman?"

I rested my hand on her knee. She crossed her other leg over it, making a hand sandwich.

A cheerful Irish brogue startled us both. "Well, John Hargrave, as I live and breathe!"

"Oh, my Lord," I gasped. "I thought I was being attacked by a leprechaun."

The banking associate laughed. He was wearing a bright green tie, a tweed coat, and khaki pants that were a size too big. "Good to see you. Outside the health club, I mean."

"Good to see you, Sean," I laughed. "You remember my wife, Jade."

"It is a pleasure," said Sean, shaking her hand. "May I offer you a delicious lollipop?" He motioned to a bowl of bank candy. "Four delicious flavors."

"Please say 'pink hearts, yellow moons, orange stars, and green clovers,'" I begged.

"And blue diamonds!" he added. "Come on in; have a seat."

"This is like a throwback, talking with a banking associate," I said, pulling out a stack of paper. "I thought this went away with ATMs and electronic checking. Humans are expensive. Machines work for oil."

"Well, don't tell that to my boss," Sean deadpanned. "He's a robot." He made a *drinky-drink* motion. "Little problem with the oil."

"Here's the deal, Sean." I pushed the papers across his desk. "We need to make a wire transfer to Belarus."

"What the blazes is in Belarus?"

"I'm buying something called bitcoin."

"What the blazes is bitcoin?"

"You haven't heard of it?"

Sean shook his head, looking over the wire transfer instructions.

"It's like a new type of digital money."

"Please don't get him started," Jade pleaded.

"And it is the most epic origin story of all time."

How Bitcoin Began

I t really is better than any superhero origin story, because it's completely true. This origin story really happened. *In this world!*

In 2008 a mysterious figure named Satoshi Nakamoto published an online paper titled "Bitcoin: A Peer-to-Peer Electronic Cash System." In it, he outlined his vision for a new type of electronic money. Imagine a world where sending money to other people would be as easy as sending email.

Electronic money had been tried in the past, but it usually failed because it's easy to copy things on the Internet: sound files, videos, classified government documents. Satoshi's idea was to marry together a few new technologies—cryptography, peer-to-peer file sharing, and blockchain—to make digital cash that was trustworthy and secure.

He called it **bitcoin**.

No one knew who Satoshi was, but since it was the Internet, no one really cared. Over the next two years he built out the technology for bitcoin, attracting a small core of programmers who helped

Bitcoin: the most well-known blockchain project, a kind of "digital money" that lets people send money as easily as sending email.

BIG DEAL

him test, develop, and refine it. In return for their work on the project, they were rewarded with small amounts of bitcoin, which at the time were worth nothing except bragging rights.

No one ever met Satoshi, because he communicated only through online forums and email. Meanwhile, the bitcoin network began to grow in size and power. Like the Internet, bitcoin ran on a shared network of computers, and "miners" who contributed computing power to the network were rewarded with small amounts of bitcoin, which were *still* worth nothing except bragging rights.

This created a virtuous circle: now miners were being "paid" in bitcoin, which created an incentive to contribute more computing power, because *what if this bitcoin became worth something someday?*

Satoshi worked tirelessly behind the scenes, fixing bugs, suggesting improvements, herding the cats. But no one ever met him face-to-face. Things grew even more mysterious in 2010, when Satoshi began transferring over all the source code to his developers.

And then he disappeared.

He left behind several personal accounts containing at least one million bitcoin,[1] which seven years later would be worth over 19 billion dollars. *And he never came back to claim it.*

Who does that? Who creates a world-changing technology, then disappears, leaving behind a fortune?

The nature of bitcoin is that people can see what's in his account—like a transparent bank vault—but no one can touch it without his permission. The nature of bitcoin is also that no bank "holds" bitcoin, so Satoshi can stay safely anonymous. His unclaimed fortune is still out there, frozen in time.

Bitcoin fanatics have driven themselves crazy trying to track down the identity of Satoshi. Everyone from conspiracy theorists to linguistic analysts have pored over every message he ever sent, trying to determine his nationality or even just his time zone.

Newsweek thought it had a scoop in 2014 when it found a guy living in California named Dorian Satoshi Nakamoto. (He denied it.) Even the world's top investigative journalists don't have a clue. Maybe Satoshi is actually a woman. Or a group. Or a government. Or aliens! No one knows for sure.

Bitcoin was the "big bang" event that started the Blockchain Revolution. Satoshi may have disappeared, but his creation is taking over the planet.

Sean was checking over our wire transfer paperwork as I concluded my story. "Interesting," he murmured distractedly.

"Think about the arc of our lives, Sean, from paper to digital," I suggested. "Do you remember sending paper mail? It took three days to deliver. Now we just use email. Do you remember paper maps? It took three people to hold one open. Now we just use Google Maps."

"All right, that's in order, then," Sean said, straightening the pile of papers. "It'll take three days to arrive in Belarus."

I blinked. "Are you snail mailing it?"

"No, that's an international wire transfer. Takes three days. How would you like to pay for it?"

"How much is it?"

"Thirty-five dollars."

"To send money to someone?" I clarified.

"To Belarus, yeah."

"Do you see what I mean, Sean? Bitcoin is going to disrupt all of this." I gestured around. "We're going to send money instantly, anywhere in the world, *without banks.* You should brush up your résumé."

"Maybe so"—Sean smiled—"but in the meantime, how would you like to pay for your wire transfer?"

"I'll use this outdated paper money," I muttered, pulling out my wallet.

"Do you know what you're doing?" he asked, looking again at the amount we were going to wire to Belarus, sight unseen. To my wife: "Does he know what he's doing?"

"Do you know what you're doing?" Jade asked me for the hundredth time.

"Look, worst case, I'm prepared to lose it all," I told them. "This is my mad money. If I wasn't spending it on this, I'd be buying stock in Google."

"And you're sending them your *driver's license*?" Sean tapped on the photocopy. "Who *are* these people?"

"I don't know exactly," I confessed. "But I did my research, and this is the place to buy bitcoin. They need my driver's license to confirm it's really me. KFC laws."

"KYC laws," Sean corrected me. "KFC is a chicken restaurant."

"We're new at this," Jade explained.

"All right." Sean shook his head. "Let me get this in progress." He walked off.

KYC/AML: "Know Your Customer" and "Anti–Money Laundering" laws require that money transmitters have proof their customers are real people, usually by requiring photo identification.

Expect to provide ID when buying bitcoin or other digital investments.

KEY TERM

Truth is, I was acting braver than I felt. Today buying bitcoin is easy, thanks to user-friendly services like Coinbase.com. Back then I had no assurance that I would ever see that money again.

"So *what* are we buying again?" Jade asked, to break the silence.

"Bitcoin. Digital currency. Think of it like a stock, if that's easier. We can always sell it back for cash if we need to."

"But the price will fluctuate, like a stock," she countered. "We could end up losing money."

"Or making money."

"It just helps to have that cash on hand. We're running a little tight this month. Our new banking client has been slow to pay."

Sean breezed back. "Done!" he said, handing me a receipt for the wire transfer.

"Hey, Sean," Jade said, switching the subject, "guess who's our new client?"

"Who?"

"Your bank!"

"What, our branch?"

"No," I laughed. "It's another division. Same bank."

"That's fantastic," he said. "You doing agency work for us, then?"

"A little project, yeah. But big for us. Writing about new banking technologies."

"They have been slow to pay, though," Jade offered.

"Nothing I can do for you there." Sean put out his hands. "Above my pay grade."

"No, I'm asking if you can increase our line of credit," she explained. "Helps us when clients are slow to pay."

"We can put in a request," he replied. "It is a fairly lengthy process, though."

"Longer than three days?" I interjected.

"We've been through it before," Jade said. "I'll take care of the paperwork."

"Sounds great. Look for it in your email." Sean stood up to shake our hands. "And good luck with that bitcon."

"Bit*coin*," I corrected him.

Then I went home to wait three unendurable days—to see if I had bought bitcoin, or if I had been bit-conned.

CHAPTER 4

The Accountant Monk

Poker Night was usually held at Kirk's house. Of the four of us, he was the bachelor.

My friend had an obsession with J. R. R. Tolkien, so his house was filled with *Lord of the Rings* paraphernalia, like the exquisite hand-drawn map of Middle-earth that covered a wall, and the shiny hobbit sword that hung over the fireplace. This was not a movie prop; this was a legit sword.

"Have you ever slain a goblin?" I asked him, touching its razor-sharp tip.

"Just an orc," he replied, handing me a can of seltzer. I toasted his beer. Kirk *looked* a little like a hobbit: he was one of my few friends who were shorter than me. He was also the spitting image of CNBC's Jim Cramer—though a kinder and gentler version.

"I just finished rereading *The Lord of the Rings* with my kids," I said. "That is some epic journey."

"Hmm?" Kirk was hard of hearing, a trait he had inherited from his mother. I was never sure how much he was getting, and how much he was missing.

"You guys in?" asked Ben. He was dealing out poker chips at Kirk's circular Vegas-style poker table. If Kirk was the hobbit, Ben was the stoic elf, and Evan was the swarthy Greek dwarf.

I sat down and threw a twenty-dollar bill on the table.

"Big spender," Ben remarked.

"Gentlemen, I am feeling generous. Tonight I am the proud owner of bitcoin."

"Oh, yeah," Evan said, shuffling the deck. "I read about bitcoin when I was getting my MBA at Wharton. It's really interesting. Like electronic cash, but it's peer-to-peer."

"No banks," I confirmed. "No government. The people own the money. Ben, that should appeal to your libertarian streak. I'll bet five."

Kirk called.

"Fold," Ben said, turning over his cards. "So what can you buy with it?"

"Well, you can't really buy anything *yet*."

"So it's electronic cash that you can't actually use as cash." Ben had a kind of knowing half smile that could be either charming or intimidating or both.

"I'm looking at it more as an investment," I responded. "Which should appeal to your investor streak."

"Sounds more like speculation than an investment."

"I'll fold," Evan said. "How many cards?"

"Give me two," I replied. Kirk also took two, and I watched him carefully. He didn't look happy, so I raised. "Five to stay in."

Kirk hesitated. "Fold." I scooped up my winnings.

"So what do you actually *have*?" Ben asked. "When I buy stocks, I get a stock certificate. Do you get a receipt or something?"

I shuffled the deck. "I have a public key and a private key."

"Like a physical key?" asked Kirk.

"No, a long string of text and numbers. Like an email address." I dealt cards as I spoke. "I can share my public key with anyone, like an email address. But I'm the only one with access to the private key. Like a password."

"What if you lose the private key?" Ben asked, knocking on the table.

"Then you lose it all." I turned to Kirk with my best Ian McKellen impersonation. "So keep it secret. Keep it safe."

Evan knocked. The bet was to me, and I sat for a moment, riffling my Vegas-style poker chips. They made a satisfying *chick-chick-chick*. The odds were good that I could walk away with the pot, even though I only had a king. But maybe Ben was also bluffing? *Chick-chick-chick.*

"Could you not do that?" Kirk asked. "It kills the hearing aid."

"Sorry. I'll bet twenty." I pushed in a stack of chips.

"I'm out." Kirk threw away his cards.

Ben scanned my face with that knowing half smile. "I'll call your twenty." He pushed in a fat stack of chips.

"Thanks for keeping him honest." Evan threw in his cards.

"King high." I put my cards in the middle of the table.

"Ace high," Ben responded calmly, showing his hand and gathering his winnings. "And the return of the king," he said, giving my cards back to me.

"It uses decentralized ledger technology," said Evan.

"Teach the schoolteacher over here," Kirk said as he cut the cards. "Decentralized ledger technology?"

"Have you ever heard of the Accountant Monk?" asked Evan.

"Do tell."

A Gift from God

Luca Pacioli was a sixteenth-century Franciscan monk who was also a genius mathematician. He hung out with Leonardo da Vinci, developed a method for teaching algebra that was easy and accessible—and, in his spare time, invented accounting.

The Accountant Monk was also a professional simplifier. Accounting had been used for hundreds of years, but Pacioli literally wrote the manual. He preached the gospel of accounting, and the other gospel as well.

Pacioli invented the idea of double-entry bookkeeping: credits on one side, debts on the other. This not only allowed us to keep count of who owed what, but it ushered in a new age of prosperity and our modern financial system. It was a monumental mathematical achievement.

Pacioli also invented the concept of an accounting ledger. You use one every time you balance your checkbook or view your online banking account. To Pacioli, a balanced checkbook was a "moral obligation,"[2] and clean books were reflective of a clean soul.

If the love of money is the root of all evil, Pacioli reasoned, then proper accounting is the root of all good. The proper allocation of value—to the places where it belongs—is how all human goodness takes root and flourishes (just as his ideas are taking root and flourishing even now in your mind).

Over the years, the accounting ledger stayed **centralized**, meaning it was owned by a person (like an accountant) or an institution (like a bank). This works fine if you have the Accountant Monk doing your bookkeeping, but not all accountants are saints.

In fact, many of the financial meltdowns we have experienced in recent times—from the Enron disaster of 2001 to the collapse of the global economy in 2008—stemmed from deceptive accounting and a lack of financial transparency. We trust accountants and auditors to tell us the truth, but *who's auditing the auditors?*

> **Centralized:** any system that is owned or controlled by a central institution (a company, government, etc.). Most present-day human institutions are centralized.
>
> KEY TERM

I can't speak for Pacioli, but since he's dead, I will. The Accountant Monk is tired of all these corrupted companies cooking the books. He wants an upgrade.

Let's call it **the Great Checkbook in the Sky**.

Accounting ledgers keep track of credits and debits, inflows and outflows of money. The blockchain is just putting those accounting ledgers online so the public can verify they're accurate. It's like open-source data.

That paragraph is the key to understanding blockchain.

With a blockchain-based currency like bitcoin, everyone can see every transaction that's been made—every bitcoin bought or sold—since the beginning of the chain. Because it's open for everyone to see, everyone can verify that the ledger is correct. Safe, honest, and clean.

Distributed ledger: like a shared checkbook, or a giant spreadsheet, open to the world. This **Great Checkbook in the Sky** is the heart of blockchain.

BIG DEAL

We're describing a **distributed ledger**, meaning that, instead of a huge paper ledger sitting on an accountant's desk, the ledger is distributed across many hundreds or millions of users across the Internet. It's like a *giant checkbook that we all balance together.*

"You're like a human Wikipedia," Kirk told Evan after he finished his tale.

"So imagine these tokens are my bitcoin," Evan continued, gesturing to his pile of poker chips. "I can send five to you, five to Ben, five to

John." He pushed piles to each of us. "This is all stored on the ledger like a giant checkbook. But no one *owns* the checkbook. It's open for everyone to see. Open-source money."

"So where does the checkbook live?" Kirk asked.

"It's distributed among millions of computers," I said, fishing for an analogy. "Remember when we used to have LAN parties?"

"Sure. Local Area Networks. Those were the best."

"Everyone would hook up their computers and play a game together. Who owned that network? No one owned it. We all just connected our computers together. Blockchain is like that. The checkbook is shared across all those computers, like a network."

"What if we disagree?" Kirk asked. "Evan says he gave us five tokens but we only got four."

"That's the beauty of the system," I answered. "It's called **consensus**. The system is designed so that the majority rules."

Consensus: the way that people agree on what's stored on the blockchain. There are different methods of achieving consensus, which we'll discuss later.

PLAIN ENGLISH
Ⓐ
Ⓑ Ⓒ

"Five-card stud," Kirk announced. "Read 'em and weep." He dealt out five cards to each of us.

"So how much is your bitcoin worth?" Ben asked, chewing a carrot.

"It's at $135!" I beamed. "I bought it at $125. Do you know how much I've already made on this investment?"

"IBM is an investment. Apple is an investment," said Ben, looking at his cards. "Bitcoin is not an investment. And neither is this." He pushed in a pile of chips. "It's a gamble."

"Twenty?" Evan said. "I'm out."

I observed Ben closely, but he was a total enigma. I was holding a pair of kings.

"I see your twenty and raise you twenty," I responded coolly.

"You boys have fun," Kirk said, throwing away his hand.

Ben didn't hesitate. "All in." He pushed in his entire stack of chips.

"Then I'm all in, too," I said. "And since my 'all in' is less than your 'all in,' I will also throw in this coffee card."

"Here we go," said Kirk.

"This coffee card has nine punches," Evan pointed out to Ben. "The tenth coffee's free."

"Well, I see your coffee card, and raise it by a Fitbit Flex," Ben said, taking off his fitness band. "The first fitness tracker worn on the wrist."

"Mmm." I scanned the room. "Well, I see your so-called Fitbit, and raise you"—I ran to Kirk's fireplace and pulled the sword from its decorative holder—"this hobbit sword!" I waved it clumsily around my head.

"Be careful with Sting!" cried Kirk.

"You! Shall! Not! Pass!" I taunted Ben, thrusting the sword down in front of me.

"Watch the table!" Kirk yelled.

I threw the sword on the poker table with a dramatic thud.

"Come on, let's get this moving," Evan said, eating a corn chip. "What do you have?"

"Pair of kings." I turned them over.

The half smile never left Ben's face. "Too bad." He turned over an ace.

"Ace high? Ace high! Ha-ha! Return of the kings!" I reached for my winnings.

Then he turned over a second ace.

"Not an investment," Ben repeated as he raked in the pot. "A gamble."

Kirk glared at me. "You owe me a sword."

CHAPTER 5

It's Raining Money

The Las Vegas Convention Center is so vast that you need to make up new words to describe it, like "hunormgous" or "gigantitanic." It is so colossal that it can actually rain inside the building. Today it was raining dollar bills.

It was probably only a couple of hundred bucks, but that looks like a lot when they're all floating down from the ceiling. I'm sure the organizers of this stunt imagined a mob of hungry convention-goers chasing the money—*real money!*—amid a riot of publicity.

Instead, there were only a half dozen attendees, looking confused.

A guy in a bright red mascot costume bounced onto the scene, scooping money off the floor and showering it back over the attendees, giving them a second chance. Most mascots smile; this one was angry. It looked like a hemorrhoid.

"Well." I looked at Pete. "This is officially the worst trade show ever."

For years we had been coming to this marketing convention, which once consumed the entire South Hall of the convention center. Now it was a sad shadow of its former self.

"Not exactly the turnout they promised," Pete agreed, "but we only need to close one deal to pay for the booth." He was the eternal optimist, exactly what you want in your VP of sales.

A few attendees were gamely picking up some lunch money from the floor, but the employees were scooping up the rest.

"How many leads we got in the spreadsheet so far?"

"Twelve," Pete said.

"Oof."

Pete peered at his laptop over his glasses. The Excel sheet was set to a zoom level of 3,000 percent. There were, like, two cells on the screen.

"Two or three highs, one medium, the rest are low probability."

I sighed. "At least we didn't pay for a mascot."

Pete laughed. "That thing looks like a zit."

The mascot, clearly frustrated, was now trying to literally pull people into the booth. Dejected, it threw up its oversized hands in frustration.

Now Pete was chortling. He took off his glasses and wiped his eyes. "Come on, that mascot is worth the price of admission."

That's because you're not paying for it, I thought.

"Speaking of price, where's our bitcoin today?"

Now my mood brightened. "Dude, it's almost at $1,000."

"A thousand dollars per bitcoin!" Pete shook his head. "Have I thanked you yet?"

"I just told you about it," I retorted. "You made the decision."

"You going to cash out?"

"It's tempting," I confessed. "When it hits $1,000, I'll probably sell some, reinvest it in Apple."

The aisle of the trade show was empty, so it gave the two of us plenty of time to talk. "A thousand dollars!" Pete repeated. "Can you imagine buying Apple stock at $100, then having it be worth $1,000 in just a couple of years? How high do you think this can go?"

"That's the $100,000 question." I was getting hungry from standing all day. "You know about the $10 million pizzas, right?" Then I launched into the story.

The $10,000,000 Pizzas

The year is 2010. Satoshi is still involved, and his bitcoin community of geeks and freaks is starting to coalesce. It occurs to one of these early enthusiasts—a fellow named Laszlo Hanyecz—that if bitcoin is to be used as digital money, someone needs to use it to *buy something in real life.*

Fittingly for a computer hacker, he buys a couple of pizzas.

Laszlo posts a message to the early bitcoin forums, offering to buy two pizzas delivered to his home. Another bitcoin user, Jeremy Sturdivant, takes him up on the challenge, little suspecting the historic nature of that experiment.

As bitcoin had no set price, they settled on an arbitrary number: Laszlo would pay 10,000 **BTC** for the two pizzas.

Laszlo (the buyer) sends the bitcoin to Jeremy (the seller) as easily as sending an email.

BTC: the abbreviation for bitcoin. Each digital currency has its own abbreviation, just like each government currency (USD = US dollars; JPY = Japanese yen; etc.).

PLAIN ENGLISH
A B C

- He enters Jeremy's public key (like an email address);

- signs it with his private key (like a password);

- then hits "Send."

He is delighted when a local pizza delivery drops off two piping-hot pizzas a few hours later. He snaps photos and shares them on the bitcoin forums, telling everyone *he bought these pizzas with bitcoin!*

A few years later, those pizzas would be worth around $10,000,000.

I know what you're thinking: *Did he at least get toppings?*

You might think he overpaid for the pizzas. But he actually showed that *blockchain currencies can have real-world value.* This was a hugely significant milestone, because it kickstarted the $250 billion digital currency market.

For years afterward, people would still ask, "But *why* does bitcoin have any value?" The answer is simple: it has value because we all agree it has value.

When some economists hear this, their heads explode. To think that people could just *invent* a currency—why, that's counter to the laws of money! "Money is a circulating medium of exchange backed by the faith of the federal government!" they cry, pushing horn-rimmed glasses back up their noses.

But haven't humans been inventing money for thousands of years?

+ In the Solomon Islands, shell necklaces were used as money as early as 1200 B.C., and they're still being used today. (One necklace is worth about $120.)[3]

+ On the Micronesian island of Yap, enormous stones are used as money: the value of each stone depends on its size, its beauty, and how many people died while moving it.[4]

+ During World War II, prisoners of war would sometimes use cigarettes as money. Modern prisoners use packets of ramen noodles, which hold their value and can be used as food.[5]

"That's not really money!" economists exclaim. "You can't pay taxes with ramen! You can't spend half a cigarette! You can't participate in capital markets with *heavy stones!*" Meanwhile, the prisoners and islanders continue to use these things as money, free from the confines of theoretical economics.

What gives bitcoin value as money? What gives anything value as money? Just two things:

♦ We **agree** it has value. I will take a payment in gold, because I know that most people agree that gold has value. The more people who agree on gold's value, the more confident I feel.

♦ We **trust** it has value. I know that gold will have value in the future, due to its long history and deep roots in the human brain. The value may fluctuate, but it won't drop to zero.

These two principles—agreement and trust—are central ideas in blockchain. They're the same principles that give any currency value—including blockchain-based currencies like bitcoin.

This is why Hanyecz and Sturdivant will go down in the annals of history. They showed that bitcoin can have real-world value. We celebrate their achievement every year on May 22: Bitcoin Pizza Day.

Why does bitcoin have value? Because pizza.

"Hello, gentlemen." A bombshell went off in our booth.

Pete and I turned to the dark-haired young woman, who was rocking a plunging tailored pantsuit, four-inch heels, and at least that much cleavage.

"I'm John," I said, avoiding a handshake. "This is Pete." There is safety in numbers.

"Lolita." Her accent was thick as Moscow fog. "We're in the booth over there." She jerked a thumb toward the next row of vendors. "How's the show?"

"Is there a trade show going on?" I joked. "All I see is vendors."

"The sellers outnumber the buyers," she agreed. "What do you guys do?"

"We're an Internet marketing agency," Pete chimed in. "How about you?"

"We're selling a new physical therapy device called the ———— Electro-Stimulator. Would you like to try it?"

A sales pitch. In our own booth! There was nowhere to run.

Pete laughed at her audacity. "What is the Electro-Stimulator doing at a marketing conference?"

"We do all the shows in Vegas," she said, smiling. Without permission, she began running two suction cups inside my collar. "The Electro-Stimulator rejuvenates tired muscles by running a small electrical current, which you control on your smartphone. See?" She connected the suction cups to her iPhone and showed us the app. This all happened in ten seconds. "Would you like to try it?"

"I know these things," I said. "They use them at my acupunct-AAAGHHH!"

"That's the maximum setting," she explained, and continued to smile as I convulsed in pain. She showed her iPhone to Pete, who laughed in disbelief.

"Let me turn it down for you." She wheeled down the dial on the screen to 4, and the sledgehammers on my shoulders subsided somewhat. "We're having a show special where you'll also get the foot sleeve, perfect for rejuvenating tired feet. And the scalp massager, which may boost brain activity."

It was hard to think clearly with AC/DC drumming on my shoulders. "How much?"

"We normally sell the package for $499," she offered casually, "but at the show we're giving them away for $249."

The worst part was not that I was being given shock treatment in my own booth. The worst part was that I was thinking, *Well, it* does *rejuvenate tired muscles.*

I shook myself from her electric spell. "We'll think about it," I told her, removing the suction cups from beneath my shirt and handing them back.

As she walked away to electrocute the mascot, I looked at Pete. "Worst. Conference. Ever."

"I cannot believe . . . That was probably illegal!"

Looking back, the day's events shocked me into an important realization: the Internet marketing industry was no longer an industry. Everyone was doing their own marketing in-house. The industry had matured, and we had to mature as well.

"Pete, we've got to find a new direction," I declared. "Let's learn everything we can about bitcoin and blockchain. This is a wake-up call."

"A 220-volt wake-up call." Pete laughed. "Hoo!"

I gazed up at the cavernous ceiling of the convention center, Pete's question echoing in my head. *How high do you think this can go?*

CHAPTER 6

Act Like You Belong

The secret to getting in somewhere you're not supposed to be? ALYB.

I was in a wide, wood-paneled lecture hall at the NYU Stern School of Business. It had the feel of a law school classroom: mahogany podium, velvet drapes, state-of-the-art projector screen. You could smell the money.

In my defense, I had tried to secure a ticket to Token Summit, but the blockchain conference had sold out months earlier. I hunted down tickets on eBay and StubHub, but the only seller I found wanted 1 BTC, which was now worth about $2,500.

So I showed up three hours early and just acted like I belonged.

If you're going to ALYB, it helps to wear a suit. I confidently breezed into the auditorium, then walked around for a few minutes inspecting the audio cabling. I ran my hands along the cords to the podium, then shouted backstage, "Tony! Tony, make sure these cables are taped down!"

I found the most inconspicuous seat in the auditorium, opened my laptop, and confidently pretended to work for three interminable hours.

Inwardly, my heart was fibrillating and my adrenals were working overtime. I started at every noise. *You shouldn't be here. You don't belong here. You're taking someone else's seat.*

I flashed back to the Bible story of Jesus preaching to his own sold-out auditorium, and the paralytic who wants desperately to be healed. His friends tear a hole in the roof of the building, then lower down the paralytic. Do we ever criticize the friends for destroying the roof? Jesus just laughs like a boss and heals the guy.

If you want to find a way in, then find a way in, I told my brain.

"Excuse me." A muscular guy covered in tattoos was standing next to me, and my heart punched the Tesla Insane Mode button. He jerked his head sideways. "Can you hold this tripod down for me?"

"No problem," I said, holding it down while he pulled his camera rig free.

"Thanks."

Finally—*finally!*—people started to fill the auditorium. I glanced at the name badges as the seats around me filled up. Goldman Sachs. J.P.Morgan. Credit Suisse. I hunkered down, opening up my suit jacket to hide that I had no badge.

Two Deutsche Bank guys sat down next to me and started talking options and credit swaps. Good-looking, trendy glasses, starched dress shirts. And they both had all their hair! Why do all the guys with all the money still have all their hair? I hated them instantly.

I began crafting an elaborate backstory for them: Porsche owners, penthouses overlooking Fifth Avenue, hot wives who spend their days working out. They all vacation together in the Swiss Alps.

"Since bitcoin is open-source," the guy to my right was explaining to his colleague, "it's free for anyone to make a copy."

His colleague grunted. "So anyone can create their own digital currency."

"Copies of bitcoin. Alternatives to bitcoin."

"Altcoins."

Altcoins. The word seared itself into my brain.

"That's like printing your own money," the colleague mused. I could hear his gears turning.

"It's just like the early days of the banking system," replied the Deutsche Banker to my right.

Printing Your Own Money

In the early days of the United States, before the central banking system was established, local banks issued their own local currency. They literally printed their own money.

Let's say you were a California settler who was paid a $5 banknote from the National Bank of San Diego. Since most of your spending was local, you'd *agree* and *trust* that the money would hold its value.

But what if you traveled to New York City? They might look at your San Diego $5 banknote with disdain, just the way New Yorkers look at everything west of the Hudson. No agreement, no trust.

The banks were supposed to hold collateral to back up their banknotes—so every $100 they issued in cash represented $100 of gold sitting in their vaults. But oversight was poor, and so-called wildcat banks sprung up, printing paper money that eventually became worthless. With no gold to back it up and no reputation to rely on, you might slap down your wildcat $5 banknote only to be told, "Your money's no good here."

Meanwhile, reputable banks prospered as the national banking system evolved.[6] Eventually the banking system was centralized, so a government dollar here was a government dollar anywhere. This enabled money to flow freely, as everyone now *agreed* and *trusted* that money would hold its value.

A similar story is playing out today in the world of blockchain. Because bitcoin is open-source (free to copy), it is easy for others to create their own alternative currencies, which we call **altcoins** (or **cryptocurrencies**). Each one works a little bit differently.

Cryptocurrency: a terrible word for digital money. First, "crypto" means either "secret" or "burial vault." Bad optics. Also: too long. Since digital currencies are alternatives to bitcoin, let's call them **altcoins**.

The best altcoins add value: they solve some real technical problem or are backed by some real-world asset. There are also altcoins of dubious value: like wildcat banks, they are cashing in on the blockchain craze. (Let's call them **wildcoins**.)

And cashing in they are. Billions of dollars have been raised by new altcoins: money created out of thin air.[7] Before you roll your eyes, remember that most money is created out of thin air: only 3 percent is paper money; 97 percent is created by bank loans.[8]

This is counterintuitive. When the bank gives you a loan, it's not "using" money it has lying around in a vault. A loan is money created out of thin air, because now you will generate more money to pay it back (with interest)—as long as you're *able* to pay it back!

Most of the time, there is no paper money exchanged. Rip up that mental model of money. It's all just numbers.

Most of us do our banking in an online account: numbers. Our paycheck comes into our online account, we pay our phone bill from our online account, we use our debit card to buy a burrito for lunch: numbers.

It's all just numbers flying around in the ether. If everyone decided to withdraw their bank accounts as paper money, the economy would collapse, because that much paper money doesn't exist. It's a fiction that we all choose to believe—and because we all *agree* and *trust* the system, it works.

So making your own money is not that hard: you don't even have to print it! But convincing people to *agree to and trust* your money is very hard indeed. You have to show that the money has value—which, in the blockchain world, means that you need to develop a strong community of believers.

Here are some of the most valuable altcoins and how they've built those believers.

Bitcoin

+ **Ticker Symbol:** BTC
+ **Market size (as of writing):** $125,000,000,000
+ **What it is:** Currency
+ **Description:** The gold standard of digital assets; the U.S. dollar of blockchain. The unspoken truth about bitcoin is that it's actually difficult to use as a digital currency. As bitcoin has exploded in popularity, it has grown slow and expensive to buy things—and its volatile price swings have made it impractical to use as cash (see **The $10,000,000 Pizzas**, page 35). This has led to the rival currencies listed below.

Ethereum

+ **Ticker Symbol:** ETH
+ **Market size (as of writing):** $50,000,000,000
+ **What it is:** Platform
+ **Description:** Programming blockchain is hard, so developers need platforms that make it easier (much as platforms like Windows make it easier for us to use computers). Ethereum is currently the standard for blockchain projects, much as English is the *lingua franca* for much of the world. While the terms are sometimes used interchangeably, Ethereum is technically the platform, while Ether is the "currency" used to run applications on that platform.

Ripple

+ **Ticker Symbol:** XRP
+ **Market size (as of writing):** $20,000,000,000
+ **What it is:** Platform
+ **Description:** If you've ever sent money internationally, you know how time-consuming and expensive it is. Ripple is a platform for banks to make these payments easier and faster, using blockchain technology. Major banks like UBS and Santander are already using it.[9] Confusingly, Ripple (the platform) runs on Ripple (the currency).

Bitcoin Cash

+ **Ticker Symbol:** BCH
+ **Market size (as of writing):** $15,000,000,000
+ **What it is:** Currency
+ **Description:** As bitcoin has grown in popularity, it has wrestled with various technical problems. Because the team working on bitcoin is not centralized (no one owns it), developers have to get majority agreement on major changes, which often results in contentious public debates. Bitcoin Cash is a "spin-off" project, designed to make bitcoin faster and cheaper to use for everyday purchases (hence the name).[10]

EOS

+ **Ticker Symbol:** EOS
+ **Market size (as of writing):** $7,500,000,000
+ **What it is:** Platform
+ **Description:** Another blockchain platform like Ethereum, though EOS has grand ambitions to be cheaper and faster. EOS investors are periodically rewarded with free altcoins from other projects launching on the EOS platform—making it a powerful promotion platform as well.[11]

Stellar

+ **Ticker Symbol:** XLM
+ **Market size (as of writing):** $5,000,000,000
+ **What it is:** Platform
+ **Description:** Another platform for exchanging money via the blockchain, like Ripple. Unlike Ripple, Stellar is nonprofit and open-source. This makes it popular among other nonprofits, and in developing markets like the Philippines, India, and West Africa.[12]

Litecoin

+ **Ticker Symbol:** LTC
+ **Market size (as of writing):** $5,000,000,000
+ **What it is:** Currency
+ **Description:** An early bitcoin clone, Litecoin has been

quick to roll out further improvements to the original bitcoin system. You might think of it as a testbed for many of the improvements proposed for bitcoin. It's meant to be faster and lighter than bitcoin, hence the name.[13]

If Satoshi's introduction of bitcoin was blockchain's big bang, then all these altcoins were the primal particles that formed in the seconds that followed. How do we decide how much they *should* be worth?

As they talked, I took out my Moleskine notebook and quietly sketched this:

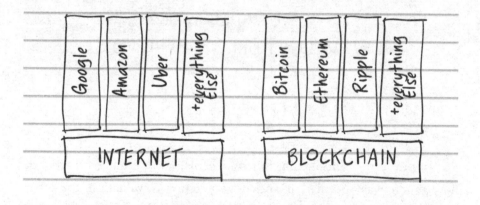

Before long, the lecture hall was packed, with people sitting elbow to elbow. The heat and humidity were stifling, but I kept my jacket on . . . until Chris Burniske took the stage.

As the paralytic was there to hear Jesus, I was there to hear Chris Burniske. A young Stanford graduate, Burniske was the blockchain projects lead at ARK Investment Management. Dressed in a suit of contrasting grays, with a faceful of stubble, he looked the part: a young Wall Street wizard.

"ARK is the only public fund manager to invest in bitcoin," he said by way of introduction. "We bought it in 2015. A lot of people thought we were crazy and buying into a Ponzi scheme, and expected bitcoin to die a long, slow death. That narrative has changed."[14]

He pulled up a slide. "Bitcoin is the number one position in two of our funds—above Facebook, Amazon, Netflix, Google, in order to give you an idea of our conviction. But in order to add bitcoin to our funds, we had to investigate it as we would investigate any stock." I scribbled wildly in my Moleskine notebook:

NEW ASSET CLASSES
REQUIRE
NEW VALUATION TECHNIQUES

To put a price on bitcoin, Burniske explained, we had to figure out how much was speculation and how much was valuation. In other words, forget the skyrocketing price: Where *should* bitcoin be valued?

"We can do a thought experiment," he continued. "Let's say bitcoin is going to take 10 percent of the remittances market. Now, the global remittances market is $500 billion. If we take 10 percent of that, that's $50 billion in value."

I quickly googled "remittances market." *Money sent by immigrant families to their relatives overseas.* International wire transfers! I flashed back to Sean the Leprechaun's three-day bank transfer. Suddenly it clicked: altcoins were so much cheaper and faster that they would almost certainly replace sending money the old-fashioned way.

Burniske was taking a thing we could measure (the $500 billion remittances market), imagining that bitcoin takes some percentage of that (10 percent), and giving it a "real-world" value ($50 billion). If we divide that by the number of bitcoin, we get a price. Eureka!

I understood that he was pulling the 10 percent out of thin air: I had endured enough business presentations to know that future sales projections were usually nothing more than educated guesses. It was the *framework* that mattered.

He was blazing a trail from the geeks of bitcoin to the cliques of big money—from the weirdos to Wall Street. Burniske was making it legitski.

NEW ASSET CLASSES
REQUIRE
NEW VALUATION TECHNIQUES

NEW MONEY NEEDS
NEW HONEY

I was listening so hard, I was sweating. Also, the room was now packed, and I think the air-conditioning had gone out. The excitement in the crowd felt barely contained, on the edge of mania.

I wrote feverishly in my Moleskine notebook:

OUR MISSION:
1. EASY TO UNDERSTAND

It was clear that even Burniske needed a translation layer. We had to make this stuff simple and fun to learn.

2. EASY TO USE

Burniske went on to explain that stocks have generally accepted valuation methods, like price to earnings ratios (P/E ratio) and earnings per share (EPS). Blockchain assets needed a similar framework.

I saw that if you could come up with these metrics, you could hire analysts to value each of these blockchain assets—like the stock analysts you see on CNBC.

3. EASY TO INVEST

It was a real aha moment: these things were real, and you could think of them like a real investor. For the rest of the day, I listened to presentations from the entrepreneurs and coders who had created their own altcoins, making notes on each:

+ **Privacy-based altcoin.** Led by funny South African guy. Big community of users, but not impressed. Pass.

+ **Cloud storage altcoin.** Just raised $30 million. Worth a look.

+ **Derivatives trading altcoin.** Founder seems unpolished. Pass.

I didn't understand half of what they were saying, but as I would later find out, neither did anyone else. We were at a strange crossroads of technology and finance. As I looked around the stuffed, stifling auditorium, I realized that half the crowd was wearing suits and half was wearing hoodies.

The audience was hanging on every word from these guys, the leaders of the Blockchain Revolution. Some of them had made overnight fortunes by launching their own altcoins and keeping a generous amount for themselves—like printing money and holding on to a vault full of it.

Blockchain billionaires—close enough to touch!

Finally, I couldn't take the heat. At the last break, I quietly made my way to the door, my head spinning with the hoopla and the hotcha. I pushed through the mob, almost at the exit . . .

"Excuse me." A gentleman wearing a suit and a clipboard stopped me. *Here it comes.*

"Yes, sir?"

"Would you mind filling out a satisfaction survey?" he asked, handing out the clipboard. "About how much you enjoyed the conference?"

"I would like to very much." I smiled.

How easy it seemed! *Easy to understand, easy to use, easy to invest.* How easy it must have seemed for the great explorer Sir Walter Raleigh: "Just sail over to South America, set up camp, then find El Dorado, the mythical city of unbounded wealth!"

How hard could it really be?

CHAPTER 7

The New New York Stock Exchange

Now I was no longer a tech writer, I was a journalist.

I had asked my team at Media Shower to launch a new website, *Bitcoin Market Journal.* Fueled by optimism that blockchain technology would wash over Wall Street, I envisioned *Bitcoin Market Journal* going head-to-head with the *Wall Street Journal.* Maybe we would even buy them out!

Never mind that we were still a tiny team working out of our home offices, or that we had only two or three writers (including me) who knew anything about blockchain. We were going to make this stuff easy to understand! Easy to use! Easy to invest!

We quickly received invitations to cover blockchain trade shows, which were springing up all over the world. Everyone wanted a "media partnership," code for "You cover our trade show, and we'll give you a free badge." Costs them nothing; costs us thousands of dollars in travel and hotels.

We usually took the deal.

That's how I found myself in Amsterdam for a blockchain trade show. How else would we learn about this stuff if not by doing our homework?

I arrived a day early, rented a bike, and spent the next few hours cycling around sunlit canals and charming old-world alleyways. My destination was this building at the University of Amsterdam, where I dropped my bike and gazed in awe.

Stand with me in its cobblestone courtyard and behold its magnificent windows and wrought-iron handiwork. Smell the scent of bread wafting out from a nearby café and let the sunshine wash over you. You're gawking in the middle of history.

This was the building that housed the Dutch East India Company: the first modern corporation, and the first publicly traded stock. This is where the modern stock market began.

In the late 1500s the public developed a taste for exotic spices such as pepper, nutmeg, and cloves. Traders imported these spices from distant lands, at great cost and great peril, with the constant threat of pirates, disease, and shipwreck.[15] ("You don't have to be crazy to sail here . . . but it helps!")

An individual investor might sink a fortune into a spice voyage, only to have a storm sink the ship. To hedge their bets, investors banded together, putting money into a shared pot and enjoying the shared profits. They were called "shares," because you *shared* in the fortunes of the company.

The real innovation was to let the public buy and sell tiny pieces of the Dutch East India Company. Now anyone—not just the wealthy— could invest in the global spice trade.

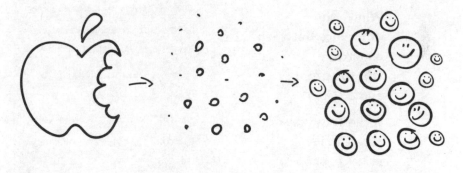

COMPANY   SHARES   INVESTORS

Think about how weird this must have been for investors. "You're buying a piece of paper?" you can picture some seventeenth-century couple arguing. "And that has value *why?*" You can be sure many of the same interrogations we hear today about blockchain investing were played out in this very building.

The stock market was a turning point in economic history. Most of us don't want to buy an entire company; we want to buy a piece. By purchasing small pieces of different companies, we diversify our risk. This unlocks a flood of new money, because the market is now open to all.

It was the first example of **tokenization**.

The Tidal Wave of Tokens

Today, blockchain tokens are taking over the world. Everything is being tokenized: not just companies but real estate, loan portfolios, luxury yachts, and so on. Using blockchain technology, we're all able to own just a piece—and that is unleashing a tidal wave of tokens.

An example will help. Let's say you own a Van Gogh painting valued at $1 million. You can sell one million "shares" of that Van Gogh as a blockchain-based token. Each "Van Toghken" is worth $1.

These tokens are bought and sold like shares of stock, but instead of being recorded at an online brokerage, each transaction is recorded on the blockchain—the distributed ledger, the open Google Sheet, the Great Checkbook in the Sky.

The investors in Van Toghken—like any investor—hope the token value will increase over time so they can sell them at a profit. Think about what this

> **What's the difference between an altcoin, cryptocurrency, and a token?**
>
> Technically, they're different. In practice, people use the terms interchangeably.
>   Let's use "altcoins" for alternatives to "bitcoin" (i.e., digital currencies), and "tokens" for anything backed by a real-world asset (real estate, fine art, etc.).

QUESTION

means for you, the owner of the painting: in order to increase the market value of the Van Toghken, you have to increase the value of Van Gogh's work.

So you hustle: you partner with museums on Van Gogh retrospectives; you commission a documentary on Van Gogh's life; you develop a Van Gogh miniseries for Netflix starring Benedict Cumberbatch.

In other words, you *add value*.

$1 MILLION
VAN GOGH

1 MILLION
VAN GOGH
SHARES

1 MILLION
INVESTORS
$1 EACH

Or let's say you're an investor in Dubai who wants to own some real estate in Manhattan. Perhaps you don't have the means to buy an entire skyscraper. The owner of that skyscraper could tokenize the building, then sell you just a piece.

SKYSCRAPER   SKYTOKENS   INVESTORS

Now, the original owner of the skyscraper is like the owner of a public company: she has an incentive to improve and renovate the skyscraper, to bring in higher-end tenants, in order to raise the value of your token. It's like buying houses in Monopoly, which generate rent so you can upgrade to hotels.

We're creating new tokens that let you buy a share of precious metals, commodities, or even major-league sports teams. (Owning a piece of the Boston Red Sox would be a different ball game than owning season tickets at Fenway Park.) **If it has value, that value can be tokenized.**

These tokens are being traded on digital exchanges, twenty-four hours a day, around the world, opening up a wealth of new opportunities for investors. We'll call it "the *New* New York Stock Exchange."

I was snapping photos of the University of Amsterdam building, when my phone rang.

"John?" It was our banking client. My heart skipped a beat.

"Sooyoung. Hi. Can you hear me okay? You're breaking up."

"We have huge problem with this blockchain work you are doing," she responded. "I need you here Friday."

"I'm in Europe," I told her. "What's the problem? We can work it out for your meeting."

"No, we need you," she insisted. "All this stuff your agency has written about blockchain. We've got to present it on Friday."

I understood the subtext: *I need you here to explain this stuff to everyone.* "Why don't we have Pete present?" I asked. "Pete's terrific."

"No," she stated flatly. "You will come. You and Pete."

"I don't know if I can even get a flight—" I began.

"Nonnegotiable," she interrupted. "Make it happen. See you Friday."

I quickly did the math. Two thousand in travel and lodging, another grand to fly back last minute, and I didn't even make it to the conference. But we needed this client, if the blockchain research was to continue.

I had no idea how that need was about to be tested.

CHAPTER 8

Never Invest More Than You Can Afford to Lose

The bank headquarters looked like a futuristic castle.

There was something vaguely menacing about the steel-and-glass skyscraper. It may have been the antennae, which gave it the appearance of a huge metallic insect, ready to strike. Swift-moving storm clouds were reflected in its opaque windows, and I felt a sense of dread.

"Did she say what we need to cover in this meeting?" I asked Pete as we checked in at the security desk.

"Nothing." Pete looked over his glasses at the security check-in screen. "What does that say?"

"You have to scan your driver's license."

"For a meeting?" Pete laughed in disbelief. Even jet-lagged and bleary-eyed, he'd retained his humor.

"This place is no joke."

We called them our "bank client," but they were a multinational asset manager that controlled over $2 trillion in wealth. Two trillion dollars is hard to imagine—it's a line of dollar bills that would stretch from the earth to the sun, *and back*—but you got a notion of it when you stepped into the conference room.

"Wow," Pete said under his breath.

The dominating impression was the massive conference table, big enough for a law school reunion, with an inlaid pattern of contrasting wood: maple, ebony, and elm. The conference table alone could be our boss.

Even more commanding was our client. Impeccably dressed in an Armani business suit and a lavender scarf, her hair and makeup flawless, she sat at the far end of the table, typing on her laptop. "Hello, John. Hello, Peter." She didn't get up.

"Sooyoung." I smiled and made my way down the table, past countless leather chairs, dropping my bags. "Hey, crazy coincidence. I saw this exact conference table yesterday at Ikea."

"Really?" asked Sooyoung, not looking up.

Pete was dying; we exchanged a look.

"Excited to be here," Pete said, unpacking his laptop. "What's on the agenda?"

"Let me videoconference them in." Pete and I exchanged another look, both thinking the same thing: *We could have videoconferenced?*

Sooyoung tapped her keyboard and a video screen covering the far wall began to glow a soft azure. It was hard not to be distracted by the pin on Sooyoung's lapel in the shape of the bank's logo—not to mention the diamond on Sooyoung's finger, which could have illuminated a disco.

Another conference room came to life on the screen. We saw three or four people, all typing on their laptops. The placement of the camera was terrible, so we were seeing them from the perspective of a small child.

"Okay, I have the compliance team from London," Sooyoung said. "Hello, everybody!" She waved cheerfully.

Everybody in London said hello, not looking up. I felt outnumbered. I glanced out the twenty-second-story window, where the sky was turning black. If I had to jump, I'd first have to break through the safety glass.

"So this is the Media Shower team, and they will talk about the blockchain article series now."

"Sure," I began.

"We have some concerns," a British bloke in a yellow tie jumped in. "There's too much promissory language. You can't say, 'You *will* own these tokens'; you can say, 'You *may* own these tokens.' You can't say, 'This is *likely* a good investment'; you can say, 'This *may be* a good investment.'"

"Got it," Pete agreed. "No problem."

"'Never invest more than you are willing to lose,'" he pontificated, "should be 'Never invest more than you *can afford* to lose.' He went through his sheaf of papers, ticking each point with a pencil. "Every article."

"You use some words too much," Sooyoung piled on. "Like 'the.' The, the, the! Why do you need so many?"

"Have you written for financial clients before?" our British pal asked. "This is all pretty standard."

"In fact, we have our own financial website, *Bitcoin Market Journal*," I responded.

"You write about bitcoin?" He leaned closer to the camera. The fish-eye Web camera gave him the appearance of a cartoon stalker.

"It's one of our areas of specialty."

"No, no, no," he laughed. "We absolutely cannot write anything having to do with bitcoin."

"We're not writing this for *you*." I rubbed my eyes. "That's our own site."

"Why do you have so many words?" Sooyoung interjected. "People on the Web don't want to read. They want it short, bite-sized."

"You're hiring us to write words," I snapped. Pete touched my arm gently.

"Bitcoin is drug money and Ponzi schemes," the Englishman continued. "Blockchain is the technology. We've got a whole team working on blockchain. Twenty-five patents. Seriously, guys, no bitcoin."

I sighed and shook my head. "You're missing out . . ." I said.

"We're not writing about bitcoin." Pete gave everyone a reassuring smile. "And we can fix the language, Sooyoung. We'll shorten the articles and take out as many 'the's as we can. All good?"

"Good," Sooyoung said. "Thanks, everybody!" She closed up her laptop and stood.

"What else?" I asked.

"That's all," she replied, smoothing her suit. "Thanks for coming in. Good meeting!"

"Uh, before we go," I asked timidly, "we're having some problems with payment."

"Did you talk with Accounts Payable?"

"My wife, Jade, has reached out several times," I affirmed. "We haven't been paid yet."

"Okay. I'll look into it. You know your way out?"

"End of the conference table, then turn left," I said, smiling.

"See you!" she singsonged. "Goodbye!"

Timing Is Everything

You may be familiar with the technology adoption curve, popularized by Everett M. Rogers in his 1995 book *Diffusion of Innovations.* It explains how technologies take hold in society.

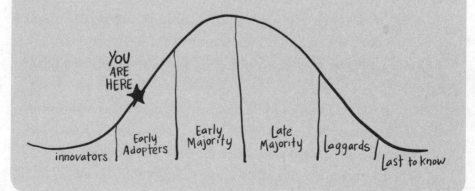

At the far left, you have the geeks who buy the first-generation iPhone. Then you have the early adopters, who buy the second generation. Then everyone else. Then at the far right, your grandparents.

A key question with any new technology is: *Where are we on the adoption curve?* In the mid-1990s, everyone predicted that virtual reality was right around the corner. I spent countless hours hacking my first PC into a homemade VR rig. Now here we are, decades later, and I'm still waiting for decent VR.

Other technologies seem to spring into the world unbidden, belly-flopping into society. Who could have predicted Twitter or Tencent?

I believe we're in the "innovator" or "early adopter" phase of blockchain. We can all agree that the technology has not yet hit the "majority." But that wave of opportunity is certainly coming, and where do you want to be when it hits?

Back in the lobby, Pete and I relinquished our badges to the security guard. "Hey, John," Pete said, gravely serious for a moment. "Never invest more than you can afford to lose."

I shook my head. "I feel like we dodged a bullet."

"I thought you were going to *fire* a bullet!" he chuckled. "Let's call an Uber. It's miserable out there." He peered at his phone through his glasses.

I took a seat on the Scandinavian lobby chairs. Across from me hung an original Banksy, spray paint on steel. "We've got to evolve, Pete."

"We could start a bitcoin exchange," Pete offered. "Those businesses are raking in the dough."

I grunted.

"Think about it!" He waved his hands in circles. "People buying and selling all these coins. Billions of dollars trading every day. Every transaction, you take a cut. You don't have to do *anything*!"

"But it's still centralized. And you have to build the exchange. That costs millions."

"So we raise the money!" Pete was undeterred. "We launch our own coin, people buy it, we use that money to build the exchange. Have you seen how much these coins are raising?"

"I think we should be doing blockchain analyst reports," I suggested. "Like Morningstar. Those guys grade all the mutual funds. They're huge. Just do that, but for altcoins."

"I think we could do custom blockchain research," Pete riffed. "Companies hire us to look at the blockchain market for, like, health care. Like Deloitte." He checked his phone. "Uber's here."

As we dashed out into the rain, my spirit felt strangely buoyant. I was convinced there was an ocean of opportunity in front of us, if only we could navigate the open seas.

The only problem: we still hadn't been paid.

CHAPTER 9

Smart-Ass Contracts

"Good morning to ya," said Sean the banker, ushering us into his office.

"Please say 'Top o' the morning t'ya,'" I pleaded.

"Top of the morning to you both," Sean responded in a stilted American accent.

Jade was not in the mood. "I'll get to it, Sean. We applied for a credit extension *months* ago." She dropped a ream of papers on his desk. "Here's all the paperwork."

I backed her up. "It's pretty ridiculous. This has taken forever. Last five years of business financials, personal tax returns, *home appraisal*? Why do you need our home appraisal?"

"As small business owners," Sean explained, "the home is used as collateral."

If our business can't pay them back, they can take our house, I said to myself. I had developed the habit of translating financial jargon into plain English.

Sean silently leafed through the paperwork. I felt exposed with this acquaintance from the gym poring over every detail of our personal finances.

"Here's the funny part . . ." Jade began.

"Funny, not funny," I clarified.

"Your bank is our client, and they are incredibly slow to pay. *That's* why we need the credit extension. We've got expenses—*which we pay on time*—but then your bank takes forever to pay our agency. So we're floating you the money. Does that make sense?"

Sean nodded, eyes still on our paperwork. "I wish I could help you with the payment, but that's—"

"Above your pay grade?" I interrupted. "Look, Sooyoung is *our* problem."

"Who's Sooyoung?" He looked up.

"Our client," I responded. "At *your bank*."

"Never heard of her."

"Of course not!" I threw up my hands in dismay. "We're just asking you to increase the line of credit—"

"Which you'll make interest on—" Jade interjected.

"—to pay our employees for the work they're doing—"

"—for *your bank*—" Jade added.

"—that you're not paying."

The irony was so thick, you could have spread it on toast. "I'm sorry you're having problems with our organization," Sean said, trying to soothe us. "And this approval has taken way too long. I can see you're good customers, with a growing business. Let me go check with my manager to get this expedited."

He whisked out. Jade and I gave each other a secret fist bump.

"This would be a lot easier if we had a blockchain-based smart contract with Sooyoung," I said.

"Okay," she replied, checking messages on her phone. "The kids have a birthday party on Saturday. Can you do a drop-off?"

"Yeah." Suddenly inspired, I pulled out my Moleskine notebook and sketched out:

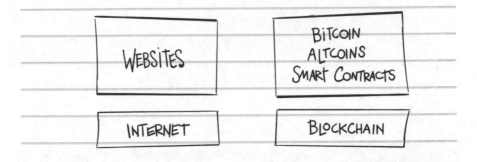

Blockchain Balloon Animals

We've seen that blockchain can allow us to:

+ send each other **money**, in the form of bitcoins and altcoins (e.g., the $10,000,000 pizzas);

+ send each other **value**, in the form of tokens. (e.g., the Van Toghken).

Blockchain can also be used to carry out *agreements* using something called **smart contracts**. We call them smart contracts because they are programmed to work without a lawyer. I will describe a smart contract as simply as possible, using balloon animals.

Smart contracts: digital contracts that require both parties to fulfill their end of the bargain. They are managed on the blockchain, without a middleman.

PLAIN ENGLISH

Let's say you hire a balloon-animal artist for your kid's birthday party. This guy is amazing. He's done balloon animals for the prime minister of Canada, and he's the personal balloon-animal artist for Bruno Mars. Very expensive, but he's not just twisting dogs. He's doing werewolves and stuff.

Because he's in such high demand, you don't know if he'll actually show up. The balloon guy might be in Hawaii at his spiritual retreat. He charges 10 bitcoin per appearance, so you send 10 BTC to a smart contract—like a holding account. You send it to an address (like an email), and it's recorded on the blockchain (the Great Checkbook in the Sky).

Let's say your balloonist doesn't show up. Jeff Bezos has hired him for the evening. The smart contract is not fulfilled, and the money is sent back to your bitcoin account automatically. The kids are disappointed, but you are able to book David Blaine instead.

Now let's say he does show up. The kids are delighted. He creates a geodesic dome of balloon animals, inside of which children can view significant moments of your child's life, lovingly constructed in balloon artistry and thoughtfully illuminated with hanging balloon fixtures.

At the end of the evening, he holds out a code for you to scan on your phone. This is an "all clear" for the smart contract to release the bitcoin to his account. It's as if you held the 10 BTC in escrow, and this releases the escrow—except that escrow requires a third party to hold the funds. This doesn't.

Could you refuse to scan the code? Sure, just like you could refuse to release an escrow payment—in which case the money sits in escrow, unavailable to either of you. With a smart contract, though, the money in dispute could be forwarded to a network of independent arbitrators who decide how much the balloon guy gets paid. (And they receive a cut of the payment for their time.)

Smart contracts are just contracts that are programmable to do anything we want.

We're just poking the surface with the balloon animal example, and we don't want it to pop. If you can picture **a digital contract** that requires both parties to fulfill their end of the bargain **without a middleman**, you have the idea.

Is everyone trustworthy? No. But blockchain systems allow us to trust people we've never met—in the same way Airbnb allows us to safely sleep on the sofas of strangers. We trust our neighbors not to run us over every time we get in a car. Blockchain is simply widening this circle of trust.

Sean strode back. "Good news," he announced. "A little problem backed up all your paperwork, but we have it resolved. I am told that we'll have your application approved in the next two weeks."

"Great!" Jade smiled. "Thank you."

"My pleasure." Sean stood up to see us out. "Hey, how did that bitcoin go, anyway?"

"It just passed $6,000." I grinned.

"And you bought it for what?"

"For $125."

Sean whistled. "Better get me some of that."

I clasped his hand in both of mine. "Never invest more than you can afford to lose."

CHAPTER 10

Blockchain or Bust

I was vomiting into a tree stump.

Vomiting is never fun, especially on a weekday. This tree stump was right next to the driveway, and that definitely made it less fun, since Martin's neighbors were probably watching.

I had been driving to meet with my adviser, when I got the call from our bank client.

"Sooyoung, hi." I put her on my wireless headset.

"John, where is our contract?"

"Sorry?" Talking with Sooyoung was like catching dinner plates. "You're looking for our contract?"

"Yeah. I need to end the relationship."

My stomach roiled. "What? Why? Is something wrong?"

"No. You do good work. We are going to bring all agency work in-house."

"I don't understand," I said, pulling into Martin's driveway and shutting off the engine. "We've been delivering incredible results . . ."

"Budget cuts," she explained. "We're looking to hire writers, though. If you have any recommendations, let me know."

"Yeah, *us*!" I replied, a little too loudly.

"When is our contract renewal?"

"End of the month," I replied. My head was swimming. "But listen. Let's find a way to work within your new budget—"

"The decision is made. Nonnegotiable."

"Sooyoung," I pleaded, "let's at least meet to discuss—"

"No need," she said, cutting me off again. "You do good work for us, but we need to make a change."

"When can you pay us? I can't tell you how many phone calls we've made."

She was ready to go. "You finish up the work, we get you paid. Fair?"

"It's not fair," I responded, tasting stomach acid in my mouth. "It's like David versus Goliath. It's not fair at all."

"Mmm." I could hear her typing away.

"We deserve better than this."

"You do good work," she repeated. "But it's time to move on. Goodbye."

I leapt out of the car and began to vomit. Poor Martin, with his beautiful home in this tony suburb of Boston—and me in his driveway, retching into his stump.

My cell phone rang. I was still wearing my headset, and I touch-activated it. "This is John," I moaned.

"Are you okay?" I lifted my head to see Martin standing at the window of his second-floor office, looking down.

"I had a bad oyster," I croaked.

"You want to reschedule? We can reschedule."

"No." I wiped my mouth. "We need to talk."

A few minutes later, revived with some hot tea, I was sitting across from Martin's two-hundred-gallon aquarium. The bubbling was soothing.

"How you feeling?" asked Martin. His hair was at the next frizz level. *New conditioner?*

"Better, thanks. Sorry about your stump."

"It's biodegradable."

"Martin, this is a difficult conversation," I began. "I think it's time we parted ways."

"Hmm." He took a sip of his tea. "Sorry to hear that."

"We're losing clients left and right," I told him. "Everyone is bringing their agency work in-house."

"The world is changing," he agreed. "Faster and faster."

"People don't just have one career anymore," I continued. "They have multiple careers. Businesses don't just do one thing; they do multiple things."

"Pivots."

"Evolution," I said. "We're all in a process of evolution. Physical, mental, spiritual evolution. If we don't evolve, we die."

"You've got to zig when everyone else is zagging." He zigzagged his fingers in the air. "And zag when everyone else is zigging."

Now that I had spilled my guts on two levels, I felt incredible relief, both physically and mentally. "You've been a good adviser, Martin. But to become a billion-dollar company, we need to reinvent ourselves."

"I don't think this has worked out as either of us had hoped," Martin agreed. "But you're going to do fine. And if you need anything at all, I'm happy to help."

"Martin, you are a class act."

"So what's your next step?"

It was the first time I had smiled all day. "Blockchain," I replied. "We're going all in on blockchain."

"Blockchain." Martin took a sip of his tea and looked thoughtful. "Remind me again: What is blockchain?"

Let's wrap up what we've learned about blockchain so far, so you can be ready to ride the wave of investor excitement in Part 2.

+ **The Internet of Value.** Blockchain can be likened to the Internet. Whereas the Internet lets us share *information*, blockchain lets us share *value*.

+ **Blockchain is a technology.** Just as the Internet is a technology upon which websites are built, blockchain is a technology upon which these assets are built:

Three categories: digital currencies, tokens, and smart contracts.

+ **The Great Checkbook in the Sky.** At the heart of blockchain is a distributed ledger, a kind of "global checkbook" or shared Google spreadsheet, that we all keep balanced together.

✦ **Bitcoin begat blockchain.** Bitcoin is the digital currency created by the mysterious Satoshi Nakamoto, who left his fortune unclaimed, in the epic origin story.

✦ **Digital currencies followed.** The explosive success of bitcoin caused a wave of hundreds of new cryptocurrencies, or "altcoins" (alternatives to bitcoin).

✦ **Smart contracts came next.** Blockchain also makes possible "smart contracts," which allow people who have never met to trust each other. (See **Blockchain Balloon Animals**, page 73.)

✦ **Blockchain assets have value.** This was demonstrated with **the $10,000,000 Pizzas** (see page 35), which kickstarted a new economy of altcoins—trading right now on digital exchanges, a newer New York Stock Exchange. (At the time of this writing, top exchanges include Binance, Bitfinex, Kraken, Bitstamp, and Coinbase.)

✦ **Anyone can invest.** The beauty of blockchain is that anyone can buy bitcoin, or the hundreds of other altcoins. While they were designed as currencies, they behave more like stocks. (We'll cover step-by-step investment strategies later on.)

✦ **Don't be intimidated.** You don't need to understand aerodynamics to fly in a plane; you don't need to be a blockchain developer to invest. Just be a learning sponge. Soak it up!

PART 2

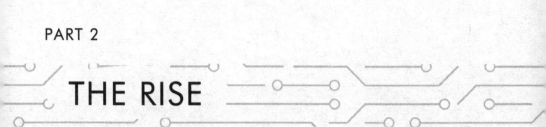

THE RISE

CHAPTER 11

History Doesn't Repeat Itself
(but It Often Rhymes)

What is blockchain?

Martin's parting words haunted me. If a seasoned tech adviser couldn't grasp blockchain, what hope did we have of making it simple enough for everyone to understand?

Blockchain for everyone became my mantra. *Blockchain for everyone.*

I was silently repeating my mantra as I informed the Media Shower team about our change in direction.

We held our team meetings via videoconference every Monday, with our editors, producers, and developers joining in from their home offices. A dozen little video windows, lined up on the screen like satellite feeds. Occasionally a dog would bark in the background.

"In the mid-1990s," I started off, "I saw the beginning of the Web, which was the greatest technology revolution of our lifetime. But the first time I saw the Web, I totally did not get it."

The Internot

Just like blockchain, it was incredibly difficult to explain the Internet in the beginning—not just how it worked, but why you'd even need it. Installing a Web browser was like genetically engineering a tomato.

I was sitting in my gray cubicle at the technology company that would later make me a millionaire. "Want to see something cool?" my coworker Ned asked me, wheeling his chair over to my desk. This was the same Ned who would be riding in the limo with me a few years later.

He loaded up a rudimentary browser, punched in an arcane address, then pulled up a homemade web page. Two words: "HELLO WORLD!" Plain black text on a dark gray background. Ned was breathless with excitement.

"This web page"—he tapped eagerly on my glass screen—"is being served off that computer"—he pointed to a black box a few feet away—"*that computer over there!*" He stared at me with a lunatic grin, like he'd discovered time travel.

"Couldn't you have connected them with a cable?" I asked.

A cable! That was my solution! Imagine the planet crisscrossed with trillions of cables, draping across mountain ranges and into oceans, connecting every device on earth. Imagine unspooling long cables connected to your mobile phone every time you leave the house. Cables! Brilliant!

It's so hard to see the impact of new technologies. Imagine if Ned had arrived with a trumpet and a powdered wig and proclaimed, "One day, twenty years hence, you will use this technology to *share photos of your food*!" Quick trumpet blast. "It will allow strangers to *buy and deliver your shampoo*!"

That was 1995. By the year 2000, dot-coms were all that anyone could talk about. Internet startups were the hottest thing on Wall Street. We went from zero to crazy in the space of five years.

While many of those Internet companies didn't pan out, some went on to become billion-dollar unicorns. In fact, some of the world's most powerful companies—the Amazons and Googles of today—were forged in that five-year crucible.

It's not always easy to recognize the beginning of a revolution, but often that's when greatness is born.

"We've seen this movie before," I concluded. "Blockchain is the sequel."

"What excites me," Pete continued, "is that we can help investors learn from the mistakes of the past." On the satellite feed, I saw him cleaning his glasses. "We can help them find the Googles and Amazons of tomorrow, instead of buying Pets.com at the height of the dot-com bubble."

"So this is it, folks," I said. "We're going all in on blockchain. Easy to understand, easy to use, easy to invest. Blockchain for everyone!"

Silence. Distantly, a dog began to bark.

"A Blockchain" or "the Blockchain"?

When we say "the blockchain," we mean it like "the Internet": to describe the larger technology.

But "the blockchain" is made up of individual blockchains, like "the Web" is made up of individual websites.

QUESTION

"Someone might want to mute," I suggested.

"So, what *is* the blockchain?" asked Wendy. "I mean, I've been reading all our work on this. But, like, how do we describe it?"

"Well, how would you describe the Internet?" I asked.

"Hmm." She thought. "I guess a place where you store information."

"And **the blockchain** is a place where you store value."

"What kind of value?"

"Any kind," Jade jumped in. Even though the two of us were sitting five feet apart, we had separate webcams. "Digital currencies, payroll data, frequent-flier points, ratings and reviews . . . anything that can be stored and quantified."

"It's hard without seeing real-life examples," Rob observed. "To explain the Internet, you show somebody email or YouTube. Is there anything we can *show*?"

"What we need are some killer apps," agreed Wendy.

My heart sank. They were right. The Web took off only because we had killer apps like email and Google. Blockchain had none of this yet. I didn't doubt the technology, but I began to doubt our timing.

"Killer apps," I said, more bravely than I felt. "That will be our first mission. Let's find the killer apps and tell the world about them."

"Or *create* the killer apps," Rob suggested.

Or die trying, I thought grimly.

CHAPTER 12

Canadian Yoda

A few weeks later I found myself in Silicon Valley at the Blockchain Expo trade show. It was a zoo.

Their timing couldn't have been better, as the price of a single bitcoin had passed $10,000 just the day before. Overnight, it was like a switch had flipped. Not just bitcoin, but the entire digital asset market—all the altcoins—were rocketing upward.

Pete and I joined the flood of ten thousand attendees pouring into the Santa Clara Convention Center, about an hour south of San Francisco. I glanced around at the name badges: NASDAQ. Bank of America. Starbucks. IBM. Heavy hitters.

This time Pete and I were visiting the exhibitors' booths, not standing in one. As the doors opened, the crowd crushed in, and I was hardly able to move.

"This is unbelievable," Pete laughed, pointing to the endless rows of blockchain startups. "Where do we start?"

"If you see that Russian woman with the Electro-Stimulator," I hollered, "run!"

We were looking for blockchain's killer apps, but instead we found a lot of filler apps. That is to say, everyone had a pitch, but no one had a product. Everyone was launching a new token, and everyone wanted you to invest.

"We're launching a blockchain prediction market," a typical entrepreneur—a young Brazilian guy wearing a purple velvet suit—pitched us. "You make predictions on anything—like who will win the next election—and you put down tokens on your prediction. All this is stored on the blockchain."

"So it's a gambling platform," I clarified.

"Prediction market," he repeated. "You can buy our tokens now, at a 50 percent discount."

"Do you have this prediction market built?" Pete asked.

"No, we are raising funds now. Our target is $50 million."

Fifty million! Twenty million! Thirty-five million! After a few of these conversations, we grew numb to the numbers.

"What's crazy is they're actually raising the money," I told Pete. We were sitting in the audience near the stage, waiting for the main presentation to begin.

"So you've got all these people buying these blockchain tokens," Pete observed, "with the goal of selling them as soon as the price goes up."

"It's like being an early investor in a hot tech company before it goes public. But instead of an Initial Public Offering, it's an Initial Coin Offering." I took a sip of coffee. "I think the ICO is our first killer app."

How to Raise $20 Billion Without a Business

We call it an "Initial Public Offering" because the public ends up paying for it.

To smell what stinks about Wall Street, just look at the IPO for Snap Inc., the social media company that offered its stock to the public in March 2017. Snap started as Snapchat, a social media app where people could send photos to each other, with the photos automatically deleted after viewing.

Snapchat quickly caught on among teens, many of whom used the app to send nude photos to each other. "Sexting, sexting, sexting. That was the narrative for the first year," said Jeremy Liew, one of Snap's early investors.[16]

Liew's involvement brought in other Silicon Valley venture capital firms, including Benchmark and General Catalyst. As Snap's user base grew, and people began to use the app for more than nude selfies, other investment firms jumped on board.

When Snap held its Initial Public Offering, everyday investors were eager to invest in the hot young company. On its first day of trading, the stock opened at $24 per share, giving Snap a total value of about $20 billion, on par with long-standing companies like Marriott and Target.[17]

Meanwhile, executives and early investors quickly sold about $935 million worth of shares.[18] To be clear, they *sold out* a portion of their shares to the general public, who *bought in*.

The problem was, Snap was burning through cash.

The company was not making a profit; in fact, its most recent year had ended with a $515 million loss. It had just ventured into hardware, launching sunglasses with a built-in camera; this product ultimately failed to take off.[19] Eventually it redesigned its messaging app, causing loyal users to quit the service.[20]

Why on earth were people investing in this company?

And this is by no means a one-off story; this is the way things work on Wall Street. IPO might stand for "It's probably overpriced." And it's overpriced on purpose, so early investors can sell back their shares at a profit.

The U.S. Securities and Exchange Commission, which is charged with regulating the stock market, even states on its website: "A firm may not sell to you IPO shares unless it has determined the investment is suitable for you."[21] In other words, the company decides who can invest.

With blockchain, we have the opportunity to democratize investing.

Imagine a cross between a startup, a Kickstarter campaign, and a traditional IPO. Like a startup, anyone can invest early in a new blockchain project. Like Kickstarter, it's crowdfunded. Like an IPO, investors receive blockchain-based tokens (like our Van Toghken) that function like shares of stock.

There were two problems with these early Initial Coin Offerings, or ICOs. First, no one was sure if they were legal. If they were stocks, they would be regulated like stocks—but they weren't stocks. Or were they? This uncertainty caused a great deal of trouble later on, as we shall see in Part 3.

Second, what were you really buying? Bitcoin had value because it had millions of users. But you're buying a token in a brand-new company, with no product and no users, and you don't even own the company?

In a perfect world, these tokens will function exactly like stock. In traditional investing, if you buy a share of Tesla, you own a small piece of Tesla. If you buy the majority of Tesla, you get to tell Elon Musk how to run Tesla. (Good luck.)

In a perfect world, if you're starting a blockchain company, you offer blockchain-based tokens, which record who owns shares of your company. Every time someone buys or sells a share, it's recorded on the distributed ledger, that Great Checkbook in the Sky.

For example, an angel investor puts in $100,000, and in return you agree to give up 10 percent of your company. Your company is now valued at $1,000,000 (or $100,000 x 10). To keep it easy, let's say you create 1,000,000 tokens, and transfer 100,000 of those tokens over to your investor's digital wallet.

The investor has all the rights of a traditional shareholder. We're working within the existing legal framework, using the model that venture capitalists and investors have used for years. But we're evolving it one step forward, onto the blockchain.

Smart stocks: stocks that are recorded on the blockchain and give you real ownership in the company. Blockchain investors must ask if a token gives ownership in the company. If not, demand to understand what gives the token value.

PLAIN ENGLISH

Think of these tokens as **smart stocks**, which can be programmed to do cool things in the future. Because it's computer code—not a paper stock certificate—these stocks will be capable of so much more, like making it easier for shareholders to organize and vote. Power to the public.

A guy shuffled onto the stage in a ball cap and jeans. "Our next speaker," he mumbled, reading off a piece of paper, "is the founder of

Blockchain News, an award-winning publisher, and entrep . . ." He stumbled on the word. "On-tep . . . on-tree . . . on-treepee . . . manure."

Pete was holding his sides, shaking silently. "Is that the sound guy?" He was wiping his eyes under his glasses.

I realized he was right: the guy running the soundboard was also making the introductions. "Maybe their emcee didn't show."

"*You* should be up there making the introductions," he whispered, pointing at the stage. I felt a little jolt of adrenaline. He was right!

"Please welcome," the sound guy mercifully finished, "Richard Kastelein."

It was my first glimpse of the man who would become our Yoda. He looked nothing like Yoda: a great bear of a man, in a black T-shirt and black pants, his jet-black hair swept up in a surfer's wave. He sounded nothing like Yoda: the Canadian accent was thick as maple syrup.

"I have some exciting news to tell you aboot this morning," Richard started off. "We just announced the acquisition of our media publication, *Blockchain News*." Applause.

"That's a good sign," I said to Pete, thinking of our own media publication, *Bitcoin Market Journal*.

"But this morning," Richard began, "I want to talk aboot community. When you consider what makes a blockchain valuable, what makes this or that token a good investment, it really comes down to *community*."

I pulled out my Moleskine notebook and wrote:

BLOCKCHAIN IS ABOUT
COMMUNITY

"I've been covering this space for aboot two years," he went on, "and I've seen the most valuable tokens are the ones owned by the most people. Which makes sense! Who wants to invest in a company with only a handful of customers? You want thousands, millions of customers."

I scribbled:

MORE USERS = MORE VALUE

"Now, there's a lot of new token offerings at the show here today," Richard continued. "But the challenge will be to build those communities. All the big coins—bitcoin, Ethereum, Ripple—they've been around for years now, they have this critical mass. They've been through the *PRO*-cess."

"Tokens take time," I whispered, writing furiously. His words had the ring of truth: as more people joined your blockchain or bought your token, you naturally had a bigger market of buyers and sellers. Then I wrote:

ACHIEVE CRITICAL MASS

"I've helped a lot of these blockchain projects get off the ground," Richard offered, "so if anyone wants to talk aboot how to build these communities of users, I'm around all day. I'll be over there, in the common area. Thank you."

"We've got to talk to this guy," I said to Pete as I applauded.

"Let's take off, eh?" Pete said, getting up.

For the rest of the day, we wandered by the table in the common area, where Richard Kastelein was holding open office hours. He sat there for hours, talking with an endless stream of blockchain entrepreneurs and executives.

Finally, I couldn't stand it anymore and just sat down at the table, uninvited. ALYB. "Hey, guys," I cut in cheerfully, "John." I shook Richard's hand as I waved Pete over. "My colleague Pete."

"Hey, guys, this is . . ." Richard gestured to the solemn young man across the table.

"Andrzej," the young man responded. I glanced at his name badge. Ukraine.

"Good timing," Richard told us. "We were just finishing up. So, Andrzej, email me if you have any questions aboot that."

"I thank you," Andrzej said with a nod. We watched him walk away.

"That is a lot of consonants," I remarked.

Richard chuckled. "Blockchain is everywhere."

"Congrats on the sale of *Blockchain News*," Pete began.

"Thanks. It's still in *PRO*-cess, but I'm pretty pleased with the sale price." He told us the number casually, like he was giving out the time. "Course, I've written nearly six hundred articles for it, staying up till two in the morning, just me on my houseboat, but not bad, eh?"

"You live on a houseboat?" Pete laughed.

"Technically, it's a yacht."

"A yacht," I repeated.

"Yeah, I love boats. Used to be a travel writer, sailed around the world. One day somebody paid me in bitcoin, and since I'm always hop-ping around between countries, it just made sense. Money without borders! I got bitten by the bug, you know, started *Blockchain News*."

"Richard, we've got this blockchain publication that's growing like crazy. How do we take it to the next level?"

"Today?" He let out a breath. "Lots of competition. Everybody's launching a blockchain site."

"What about launching your own token?" I asked. "How much to do that?"

"These token sales are getting expensive," he confided. "Legal, marketing . . . I'd plan on a million dollars, easy."

"A million to launch," Pete clarified, "but then you can raise, like, $50 million, right?"

"Sure, if you can stand out." He gestured at the booths all around us. *Everyone* was launching new tokens. Printing money. "It's getting so expensive," he continued, "that some of these guys aren't just doing a token sale. They're doing a presale to raise the money to do a sale. Sometimes a pre-presale."

Now I didn't feel we were too early; I felt we were much too late. The noise, the crowd—the *chaos*—were suddenly overwhelming. "What's your best advice for someone new to this game?" I asked.

"*Build a community*," he emphasized. "Build a community, then find a way to add value. Blockchain is like a big, wide-open field. There's just, like, fertile soil waiting to be tilled." He crumbled imaginary soil in his fingers. "And have a thick skin."

In my Moleskine notebook, I wrote down in all caps: "BUILD COMMUNITY." But as I would find out shortly, what I should have also written was: "THICKEN SKIN."

CHAPTER 13

For the People, by the People

I was giddy to kick off our first blockchain investor meeting. The price of bitcoin was nearing $20,000, and my initial purchase had multiplied more than 150 times. It wasn't just bitcoin: anything blockchain was gushing cash. Our timing was perfect!

"Let's get this started!" I announced, turning on the overhead projector, and people began filling seats.

"Welcome!" I began. "I'm John Hargrave from *Bitcoin Market Journal*. First, a big thank-you to TechLab for hosting! Benedict, the community director, will say a few words."

Benedict took the mic. "Welcome to TechLab, the best technology coworking space in Boston." He gestured around at the coffee bar, foosball tables, and motivational posters reading *You Got This*. "One monthly membership lets you join our community of freelancers, remote workers, and tech startups."

"This space is amazing," I enthused, looking around. "It's like working at Google, but you don't have to be smart." Some laughs.

"See me afterward if you'd like to join." Benedict handed the mic back.

"Transparency is important," I told our few dozen attendees, "so let me begin by telling you that I'm an investor in bitcoin, Ethereum, and Ripple. How many of you own bitcoin?"

Most of the hands went up.

"Bitcoin is the gateway drug," I said, and got a laugh. "Let's introduce ourselves and how we got into blockchain," I suggested. "I'm curious to learn more about the 'average' bitcoin investor."

I quickly discovered there *was* no average.

There was Diane, the work-from-home mom; Travis, the licensed real estate agent; Hanaan, the technology entrepreneur; Carl, the project manager; Jennifer, the student; Rob, the doctor. There was Peter, the former male model who had made a successful career pivot into finance.

And me, the comedy writer turned blockchain investor. I swallowed.

"What does a blockchain investor look like?" I began, pulling up my PowerPoint. "Look around! Blockchain investors are all over the map. Literally! We are all ages, from all walks of life, all regions of the world, male and female, crazy and sane." A few chuckles.

"But personality-wise, we share three things in common:

+ **We are early adopters.** We are willing to jump in before everyone else—which is how many successful investors earn their wealth. We are innovators and pioneers.

+ **We are tech-friendly.** Investing in blockchain requires a certain level of tech proficiency. We love technology. We embrace our inner geek.

+ **We are lifelong learners.** We love to learn! Being addicted to learning is the one addiction I can heartily recommend.

"Does this capture who you are?" I asked. Nods of agreement. I advanced my slide.

"We're at a singular moment in history, because blockchain is changing the rules of investing. And the rules need changing!

✦ Everyone should be able to invest in the companies they care about—not just the rich.

✦ Everyone should be able to invest any amount—no minimums.

✦ Everyone should be able to invest at the same time—no early-bird discounts for the privileged.

"The principle of democracy," I continued, "is one person, one vote. Investing is just voting with your money. *Shouldn't the rules be the same?*"

Silence.

"So, uh . . . one sec." I turned to Pete and whispered, "Did we bring the handouts?"

"I thought *you* brought them."

"Let's . . . let's open our laptops," I wobbled, "and check out the website for our first blockchain project, Swytch. Now, who read through their materials?"

A couple of people raised their hands.

"Look in my bag," I whispered to Pete.

"Swytch is a solar token," offered Brandon, a young man in his twenties who had introduced himself as an "independent blockchain investor," which meant that had he bought enough bitcoin to quit his job and just do investing full-time. "You earn Swytch tokens for generating solar power."

"I saw Swytch as being more like carbon credits," offered Henry, a former banking executive. "Your solar panels generate electricity, which you can sell on this solar marketplace, like carbon credits. All the transactions are recorded on the blockchain, so no company or country owns this data—we all do."

Pete shook his head. *No handouts.*

"Other thoughts?" Silence. I couldn't believe no one else had read through the materials. *Come on*, I told myself, *you've done improv. Roll with it.*

"Yes, and," I began, "I'm pretty sunny about solar. Let me tell you a story."

Switching the World to Solar

A few years ago, my wife and I installed a massive solar array on the roof of our house. We were lucky that we had a perfect location: southern exposure, a large, flat roof, plenty of sunlight.

But making the decision to invest in solar wasn't easy. We agonized over it for several years. It's expensive. It's time-consuming. And it turns out the sun is only going to be around for another five billion years.

We invested anyway, and we've never looked back. You have no idea how good it feels to generate your own solar power. You wake up on a sunny summer day and see the sun is shining: it's like a big, warm paycheck in the sky.

It feels amazing to get the "negative energy bill," where you are selling power back to the electric company. Every day those panels are minting money. Zero effort. The sun does the work!

We love solar so much that we recently switched to an electric car. This was also a huge decision. The first question everyone asks is: "But what's the range?" Everyone is afraid of running out of electricity, like people must have worried when switching from horses to cars.

You're not going to run out of electricity. Ninety percent of your driving is short hops. If you need to take a cross-country road trip, that's why you have a second car. At night you just plug in your electric car like you charge your phone. Your car is a device.

So now the sun is powering our home, our devices, and our car. We run on the sun. Once you make the switch, you realize solar is just common sense. Why would you do it any other way when the sun is totally free?

I would love a little box that attaches to your solar array, generating a blockchain token every time you generate a kilowatt-hour of electricity. Let's call it SolarCoin. These tokens would have real value, because other people—like your neighbors—could buy your electricity using SolarCoin. (Electricity loses juice as it travels long distances, so buying fresh local electricity is cheaper.)

The idea is similar to carbon credits, which are used to incentivize companies—or entire countries—to reduce pollution. Countries that invest in reducing greenhouse-gas emissions can sell their excess carbon credits to countries that pollute more. Carbon credits work.[22]

As I look up on our roof, I think about how much solar energy goes unused. The potential power is virtually unlimited, and it just gets soaked up by trees and Italian tourists. The power struggles over oil—at such a price of blood and treasure—seem ridiculous when you consider the alternative of investing that willpower into solar power. Let's put our energy into energy.

Energy consumption: Bitcoin and other altcoins require "mining rigs," or high-powered computers, to run the distributed network. These consume massive amounts of electricity.

Reducing this energy consumption is one of the primary challenges facing blockchain today. (We're working on it.)

"Think of the data!" said Kuppu, a product manager. "Storing all that solar data on the blockchain can show us which regions use the most electricity. Or seasonal variations. Or changes over time. All these new businesses that will spring up to analyze that data for companies and governments."

"Right." I pointed at him. "We'll be able to build new solutions to serve—or conserve—power where the world needs it most."

"One of our biggest problems in blockchain is **energy consumption**," said Frank, an engineer. "The amount of energy required to run bitcoin alone could literally power a small country.[23] So I'm skeptical. Seems like these energy tokens will just devour more energy."

"Well, what if we make more than we take?" I asked.

"Power drives power," said Kevin, a college student majoring in economics. "Power consumption drives economies: you need electricity to make things. Power causes wars: when you don't have electricity, you fight for oil. Power runs the world: when you're sitting on power sources, you own the planet. But everyone has the sun."

Now we were cooking. Some people loved the project; some people hated it. But everyone could buy into it if they wanted to.

"How many of you would personally invest in this blockchain project?" I asked, and we took a show of hands. "And how many would pass?" Pete charted the stats quickly in Excel and projected the results on the screen.

"Lots of questions," I concluded. "So why don't we ask the man behind the project? *Ladies and gentlemen, Andrew Pearsons, managing director of Swytch!*" With a flourish, I stretched my arm toward the young man who had been sitting silently in the corner. He smiled and waved.

In my mind, this was the big reveal. I pictured a stage, a live studio audience, and a triple spotlight sweep over to Andrew. A band would start playing and the audience would gasp. Every episode would have a little surprise moment like this baked in.

Instead, I heard a few groans. Some people had really been trash-talking the project.

Andrew was gracious. "Blockchain has the power to make energy production cleaner, cheaper, and more resilient." He smiled. "At Swytch, we're building a better, blockchain-based marketplace for solar energy, which will encourage more people to switch to solar."

"Imagine switching the entire human race onto solar in one generation," I concluded. "*In* this *generation*. With blockchain, this is within our reach. Thanks for coming, everyone."

Silence.

"We're done now," I clarified.

People began to mill about, and Benedict came over. "Good turnout," he said, shaking my hand. Benedict was in his thirties, almost impossibly good-looking, with incredible teeth: flawlessly white, precision set, like they had been manufactured in a lab.

"Well, blockchain is hot," I responded, too self-conscious to smile.

"That's why I wanted to talk. We're opening a new TechLab office downtown," he told me. "Our biggest yet. Eight floors."

"That's insane."

"Yeah. Amazon has already taken one floor. Microsoft is just about to take another."

"So these companies can just spin up a Boston office by renting out the floor. You guys take care of everything."

"Bingo." He pointed at me.

An idea struck me. "Hey, why don't you dedicate an entire floor to blockchain?"

"That's just it," he said. "I'm in charge of filling up this new office. I think we could partner up."

"It's like a blockchain incubator," I said, nodding.

"All these blockchain startups, blockchain investors, blockchain companies . . . This could be the place."

"Sold," I said. "No-brainer. This is good for Boston. Good for block-chain."

"Let's talk," he said, giving me his card and flashing me his Tom Cruise smile.

"Let's sell!"

And so the night ended even giddier than it began. Out of the home office and into the blockchain! Our first real partnership! Then I checked my email.

To: John Hargrave
Subject: Your "investor" event

Mr. Hargrave: as a Certified Financial Planner who has been asked by several clients about bitcoin, I decided to see for myself what all the hype was about. I was so disgusted that I left early.

It is extremely irresponsible and DANGEROUS to give out financial advice. You have no credentials. No disclaimers. No warnings.
Its [sic] obvious bitcoin is in a bubble, and your "investors" are going to lose it all. Because they're not investors, they're speculators.

Your [sic] exactly the reason that we study for over 1,000 hours to be a CFP. I know that was your first meetup. I hope it will be your last.

I found Jade cleaning up pizza boxes. "How much did we spend tonight?" I asked.

"About $1,000," she said. "Food, drinks, rental, printing . . . although some of the printing can be amortized." She calculated. "Nine hundred sixty-eightish. I thought it was good, though."

"Read this." I gave her my phone.

"Well, he has a point." She handed back my phone and kept cleaning.

The email really soured my mood. Even with the soaring price of bitcoin, it brought me down to earth with a nagging doubt. It was the question Ben had originally posed at Poker Night: *Was this all a gamble?*

CHAPTER 14

Investing vs. Speculating

"Well, gentlemen, bitcoin closed at $20,000 today," I said, tossing a $5 bill on the table.

"And you're buying in for five?" asked Kirk.

"That's all the cash I have," I admitted. "Everything else is tied up in bitcoin."

"I was reading that they launched bitcoin futures today." Ben sat down and cracked a beer. "That probably drove the speculation."

"Today you call it speculating. Tomorrow you'll call it investing." I pushed my ante into the pot. *Assuming it works out.*

"Are you familiar with the Railway Mania of the 1840s?" asked Wharton-educated Evan, dealing out hands. "People in Great Britain got so excited about the potential for railroads that they drove up the price of railroad stocks to stratospheric heights. Then you had these powerful railroad capitalists that were manipulating the market behind the scenes and paying off journalists to build up the hype cycle. Then, when it came crashing down, all these middle-class families lost their life savings."

"Sounds familiar," said Ben, looking at me with his half smile.

I knocked. Kirk knocked.

Ben pushed in a poker chip. "I've seen so many guys make these huge trades, putting their life savings into some overhyped stock. A lot of times, they win. Then they make another big bet, and the next time they lose. They should be at the casino, where at least you get free drinks." He took a sip.

"I've been reading up on bitcoin." Evan called Ben's bet, and I followed. "There was this guy who made a fortune in bitcoin, then lost it all."

"Like, spent it?" asked Kirk, folding.

"No, he *literally lost it*. Donated the hard drive to Goodwill."

"Pretty good donation," Ben said, showing his cards.

"Not without the private key," Evan said, taking the pot. "Irretrievable."

"Which is the word I want on my gravestone," I threw in.

"Ante up," said Kirk, riffling cards.

"I will tell you that investors are not doing their due diligence," I admitted. "We do these meetups, and no one is reading about the projects beforehand."

"Well, there are no metrics to measure by, are there?" said Ben, chewing a handful of granola. "I'm spending all day looking at P/E ratios, earnings per share, all these metrics. What do you have to measure bitcoin?"

"Price," I responded.

"But what is price? There's nothing to measure its value *against*. It's just comparing price against price. It's a hall of mirrors."

"Texas hold 'em," Kirk announced. "Playing with jokers."

"Do you guys know about Charles Dow?" asked Evan. "He was this financial journalist at the beginning of the stock market. They had the same problems. Lots of speculators. No good yardsticks. So he created some simple metrics to measure the market as a whole. He came up with the Dow Jones Industrial Average, which was just the average of the twelve big industrial company stocks. Financial genius."

"Alexa," Kirk called out. "Who knows more, you or Evan?"

"Sorry, I don't know that one," Alexa replied.

"What did she say?" Kirk asked me, leaning closer with his ear directed at me.

"She said Evan."

"Alexa," Kirk called again, "play some dance music."

David Bowie's "Let's Dance" started playing on Kirk's Alexa device.

"Now, *this* was the financial genius," I said, tossing in my cards. "Did you ever hear about the Bowie Bond?"

Tokenizing Music

In 1997 the British rocker David Bowie introduced a novel investment vehicle called the "Bowie Bond." In collaboration with the investment banker David Pullman,[24] the Bowie Bond offered an interest rate of 7.9 percent over ten years. Let's explain in plain English how this worked.

As an investor, you'd buy a Bowie Bond, backed by the future earnings on David Bowie's music. Let's say you invested $10,000: a "loan" to David Bowie and his bankers. Using the royalties from songs like "Space Oddity," they would pay you 7.9 percent interest until the bond matured, then pay you back the $10,000.

The bonds were given an investor-grade rating from Moody's,[25] and ultimately raised $55 million,[26] which Bowie used to buy back rights to his old recordings, as well as invest in a number of new businesses.[27]

Bowie was opting for a guaranteed up-front payment instead of future royalties. Bowie invested his payout in new Internet companies—just as file-sharing services like Napster began to decimate the music business. He jumped from the building as it exploded, only to land on a hovercraft.

David Bowie **tokenized** his music. He showed that his music had future value, then he packaged it in a way that let investors buy just a piece of that future value. Bowie didn't invent the concept of bonds, but he showed that even something as ephemeral as music could be split into fractional shares.

Think about how weird this must have been for investors. "You're buying a piece of Bowie's *music*?" you can picture some guy asking his business associate. "And that has value *why*?" You can be sure many of the same arguments we hear today about blockchain tokens played out with the Bowie Bond.

"That's not tokenization," Ben stated calmly. "That's a bond."

"And this is a bet," I countered, pushing in a fat stack of chips.

"Out," Kirk said, tossing in his hand.

"I see you"—Ben's half smile was turning into a 53 percent smile—"and raise."

Evan folded.

I was not expecting this. Spread out on Kirk's Vegas-style table were five cards: jack, eight, four, two, ace. I peeked at my hole cards: a jack and a joker.

"Alexa," I called out as a bluff, "what are the odds of a flush?"

"Sorry, I don't know that one," Alexa responded.

I riffled the Vegas-style poker chips. *Chick-chick-chick.*

"Ow." Kirk pointed at his hearing aid.

"Sorry." I pushed in my chips. "All in."

"Now we've got a game!" Evan smiled, dipping a carrot into hummus.

"All in," Ben said as he matched me. It was clear his chip stack was bigger than mine.

"I'd like to buy more chips," I told Kirk.

"You can't do that."

"You could throw in some bitcoin," Ben suggested.

"Bitcoin is for investing," I reminded him, "not gambling."

"All right, let's see what you've got," Ben said.

"Not yet." I kept the Elf locked in my tractor beam gaze. "Kirk, get the ferret."

"You can't bet Mr. Softie!" Kirk cried.

"Kirk," I growled, "*get the ferret.*"

There were a few excruciating minutes of silence, broken only by the sound of Evan munching carrots. Ben and I were locked in an unblinking stare-off. I was hunched forward like a cobra, ready to strike. Ben casually draped one arm over the chair, the very picture of insouciance.

From the other room came the clanging of metal. "Mister *Softie,*" Kirk called out, exasperated. A stack of shoeboxes fell over.

Evan let out a snort, but I remained stone-faced, waiting for Ben to blink. His face was as inscrutable as a Russian war cipher.

"That's a good boy," said Kirk, placing his ferret in the middle of the table. The serpentine rodent scampered wildly about, demolishing the neat stacks of chips and cards before leaping from the table and making a run for it. "Mr. Softie!" Kirk called.

"All right," said Ben, his half smile never breaking, "I see your ferret and I raise you a human being. I bet Evan."

"I see your Evan, and I call you a Kirk."

"So . . ."

"All human beings are created equal," I said, "so you can call with a ferret."

"Come on," said Evan. "Turn 'em over, guys."

I set down my cards faceup. "Three jacks, ace kicker." I held my breath. Three aces would beat my three jacks.

"Interesting." Ben was moving in exaggerated slow motion.

"What do you have?" demanded Kirk.

"Interesting," repeated Ben. "Because that's also what I have." He put down a jack and a joker.

A tie. We split the pot.

It was the last time we would split it.

CHAPTER 15

The Comedy Economist

"Welcome to Boston's Blockchain District," I said with a theatrical sweep of my hand. "It used to be called the Financial District, but we renamed it yesterday." I allowed the group a moment to take in the magnificent fifteenth-floor view. "This way!"

We ushered the team of financial executives and hedge fund managers through our new space at TechLab. "Through this doorway, my friends, is the beating heart of our blockchain incubator. We call it a blockchain incubator because we're growing babies on the blockchain.

"Here's our ticker showing real-time quotes on bitcoin—looks like it's down today—and the top ten altcoins. Over here we have a blockchain consulting firm, a blockchain investing firm, and a blockchain trading firm. These guys have twenty-five monitors set up in here. They'll have tumors by the end of the week.

"Here's our new TV studio, and down here is Blockchain Startup Row. As a prank, these guys filled this office with Jell-O, floor to ceiling. Terrific mess. That didn't really happen, but I wish it did. And . . . here we are, the Blockchain Briefing Room."

I had been giving this tour twice a day for the past month, and we had sold out the entire floor of TechLab before opening day. Usually the tour got more laughs.

"Blockchain." I started my presentation on the overhead projector. "It is building a new generation of wealth and power, a new generation of blockchain billionaires. We call them 'whales' because of their ability to make a splash in digital currency markets. Also, many of them have large blowholes."

Crickets. In my head, that killed. In the room, it died. The guys from Fidelity were staring at their laptops.

"Let me show you an intro to blockchain from HBO's John Oliver." The talk show host had recently done a very funny segment on bitcoin, and I showed them an excerpt on the projector screen.[28] The sound wasn't working correctly, and the video kept buffering. No laughs.

"Blockchain is changing your jobs, because it's changing money. And speaking of changing money"—I pulled out my wallet—"can any of you break a twenty?" This was hilarious just hours earlier. "No? Only hundreds?"

"I think I have it," said a hedge fund administrator in the back of the room, counting out some bills.

"Never mind." This was like being slapped with a wet trout. "Let's talk about the changing nature of money." I pulled up a slide with a picture of poker chips.

"Here's a thought experiment. Imagine you live in a country where the official currency is poker chips. Now picture your poker chip economy going through massive inflation. Last month a sandwich cost two poker chips; this month it costs four. That car you were going to buy for a thousand chips is now selling for two thousand.

"After a few years of this, you're struggling to survive. You can't afford to eat. So the government starts minting new colors of poker chips, each worth a thousand times the value of the old one. That should solve it, right? Now the two-chip sandwich costs two thousand chips, but all the chips are worth a thousand times as much. It's still just two chips!"

"Doesn't work that way," said the hedge fund guy, looking down at his phone.

"Exactly. The deli owner is still not making enough to cover his costs, so he raises prices again. Now the two-thousand-chip sandwich becomes a two-million-chip sandwich. Eventually the sandwich gets so expensive that the deli owner starts weighing the money instead. Now a sandwich is worth two pounds of million-dollar chips, which makes it a trillion-dollar sandwich. Same sandwich, but no pickle."

"We get it," said the hedge fund guy. "Hyperinflation."

"Right. And what do you do when you're in an economy with hyperinflation?"

"Move somewhere else!" This got the first real laugh of the day. *Hedge Fund gets the first laugh?*

"How?" I asked angrily. "How do you move when you have barely enough money to buy a sandwich?"

"You have plenty of money; it's just not worth anything."

"Right." I struggled to maintain control. "So now, when you get paid, you convert your poker chips into bitcoin. They're held in your bitcoin account, your digital wallet, until you need to buy something. Then you head over to your local coffee shop, where you meet with the chipchanger.

"The chipchanger is easy to recognize, because he sits in a corner smoking cigarettes and wearing a fedora. He buys your bitcoin—you transfer it to him like email—and he gives you poker chips at today's market rate. This lets you buy groceries or pay taxes. Even if the government outlaws the chipchangers, citizens will just start trading bitcoin with each other. *The citizens will work around a bad government.* The government will find it is powerless to stop the flow of money out of its own leaky financial system."

"This is exactly what's happened in Venezuela," piped up one of the executives from Fidelity, who I would later learn had already bought bit-coin. "Their currency is so devalued that they weigh it on scales instead of counting it out."

"Didn't Zimbabwe issue a hundred-trillion-dollar bill?" asked one of her colleagues.

"Yes and yes," I responded. "You can bet that the citizens of these countries will be the first to switch over to digital currencies." I pulled up a slide:

Country	Hanke Annual Measured Inflation Rate
Venezuela	48,072%
Iran	260%
Turkmenistan	128%
Argentina	122%
Sudan	103%
Turkey	90%
Yemen	66%
Zimbabwe	46%
South Sudan	37%
Liberia	32%
TARGET INFLATION RATE FOR HEALTHY ECONOMIES[29]	2%

"This list comes from the 'Troubled Currencies Project,'[30] the brainchild of Professor Steve Hanke at Johns Hopkins University. He studies countries that aren't able to maintain a stable national currency, where the money ends up like poker chips. But it's hard to find reliable exchange rates for these countries, so Hanke also uses black market exchange rate data from the 'chipchangers.'"

"How does a nation's currency end up as worthless poker chips?" I asked.

"War," piped up Hedge Fund.

"Corruption," offered the Fidelity executive.

"Lack of national infrastructure," said her colleague.

"It all boils down to a *break-down of trust*," I pointed out. "When citizens lose faith in their government, they lose faith in their government's currency. That is the foothold that digital currencies need, the crack in the pavement that allows them to take root and ultimately flourish."

"People are losing trust in government," I continued. "We are losing trust in our financial systems. The task before us is to build trust in this new class of digital currencies. Bitcoin is global money, beyond the reach of any government, to help the **unbanked**.

Unbanked: citizens without access to a traditional financial institution, whether out of distrust or inaccessibility.

Blockchain is making financial services available to the unbanked by bypassing the banks altogether.

"As we build this trust"—I pulled up my closing slide—"we might just become blockchain billionaires ourselves. Here is $10,000 invested

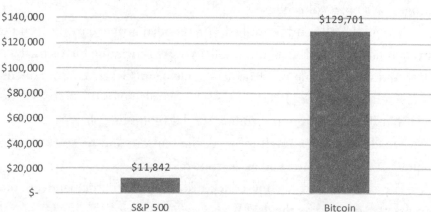

$10,000 Invested in 2017

Returns from 1/1/17 through 12/31/17. Sources: Yahoo Finance, CoinMarketCap.

in the stock market at the beginning of 2017," I explained, "versus that same $10,000 invested in bitcoin."

"Look," said Hedge Fund, finally putting down his phone, "bitcoin is a bubble. This crazy price run is driven by speculation, fear, and greed. It's going to come crashing down. The people in your poker chip world are just switching one unstable currency for another."

For the first time all day, I was quiet. Then: "Well." That was my witty comeback. "Are there any other questions?"

Most of the executives left quickly afterward, which was disappointing. *Probably to work on their golf swings*, I thought, *or to stock their new wine cellars.*

Benedict from TechLab was working at the front desk. He flashed me that hundred-kilowatt smile. "How'd it go?"

"We had quite a turnout," I replied, focusing on the positive.

"You sure did. Which is why I wanted to talk."

"You want to move these training sessions to a bigger space?" I asked, hopeful.

"No," he said. "Actually, the opposite. It's getting hard to manage all the people coming to these events. We've got to check them in at security, make sure they get out after your meeting. Some people are just hanging around all day without paying for a day pass." He smiled winningly. "It's not a coffeehouse."

"I would think you'd be thrilled," I responded, irritated by the turn the day was taking. "Look at all this publicity we're generating for TechLab."

"And we appreciate it." Benedict's smile never flickered. "But remember: you don't own the place."

"No," I replied, "but remember: we did fill up this place."

Benedict let out a laugh to break the tension, and he stuck out his hand. "We all good," he said as we shook.

The conversation left me concerned, because the demand for our events was growing by the day. *We headed for trouble?*

CHAPTER 16

The Blockchain Investor Scorecard

After the tough crowd at our Blockchain Briefing, you better believe I was nervous to speak to an audience of Swiss investment bankers.

"Our next speaker," announced the emcee, "is the chief executive of Mind Shower. Can I introduce to you the man who predicted *crypto will never last*. Please welcome John Hargrave."

What? When did I make such a prediction? It was as if he had just thrown me into a pile of dog crap, then pushed me onstage. *Do I correct him? Do I clarify?* All this went through my mind in two seconds, like the spinning wheels of a slot machine, before landing on my answer: *Ignore it.*

I looked out at the large room, which was filled to capacity. I was speaking at a convention in Zug, Switzerland, a region that was quickly establishing itself as the Silicon Valley of blockchain, thanks to its abundant wealth and forward-thinking government. I swallowed.

Everyone looked so *good*. Starched shirts, pressed suits. My German was laughable; their English was impeccable. I felt I had landed on a planet where bankers were the dominant race; one of them would ultimately trap me in a cage and keep me as a pet. *Monkey Boy is funny!*

I began a riff that would eventually become the Blockchain Bazaar.

The Blockchain Bazaar

Here's a thought experiment. Imagine you're walking through a crowded market that we'll call the Blockchain Bazaar. In every stall are vendors selling tokens. Some tokens cost a fraction of a penny, others cost thousands of dollars. The tokens may or may not have some underlying value.

"Buy some JewelCoin!" yells one vendor. "Own a piece of JewelChain! Jewels on the blockchain! Real jewels!" He is surrounded by goblets of glimmering jewels, and pours a gem-encrusted chalice of diamonds into a golden bucket. "Backed by the Queen herself!"

"Pay him no mind," says a well-dressed woman in a conservative suit. "Can I interest you in some AutoCoin? We have partnerships with five major automakers to put data from self-driving cars onto the blockchain. We call it AutoChain. It's a magnificent opportunity."

"Check out CannaCoin," breaks in a third vendor, a young guy with frizzy hair and an overbite. "It's a blockchain of blockchains, a derivative of derivatives. It's a chain of coins in chains. It's a chili cheese chain." He gazes into the distance. "Okay, it's a weed token."

How do you make sense of this madness?

Now imagine you walk through the bazaar with a simple score-card. The scorecard tells you the questions to ask, and you get to keep asking until you get an answer in plain English.

For example, there's a line on the scorecard labeled "Partnerships." You approach the JewelCoin vendor and start grilling him.

"You say it's backed by the Queen herself," you ask. "Do you mean Her Royal Majesty, Queen Elizabeth II?"

He looks taken aback. "Well, not *that* queen, mate. You know, the other one."

"Queen Margrethe II of Denmark? Queen Latifah? The Dairy Queen?"

He chuckles, looking from side to side. "Not exactly, mate."

"Who, then?"

"You know." He lowers his voice. "The drag queen."

The scorecard lets you rate each category on a scale of 1 to 5 stars. Under "Partnerships" you mark a 1.

Next, you go to the AutoChain lady. "You say you have five auto companies partnered up," you remark. "Who are they?"

"Ford, Nissan, Toyota, Honda, and General Motors."

"Impressive," you respond. "And what kind of partnerships are these? Signed partnerships?"

"All five have agreed to start sending test data to our blockchain. That will give us our initial data to develop new products."

"And these are signed partnerships?" you repeat.

"Three are signed, two are verbal commitments."

Even three major automakers is a strong base of partnerships, so you take out a new scorecard and rate AutoCoin a 5 in the "Partnerships" category.

Finally, you visit CannaCoin. "Do you guys have any partners lined up?" you ask.

"Cheech and Chong!" he chuckles.

On your scorecard, you mark a 4. For a cannabis token, Cheech and Chong are pretty good partners.

"Most people wander through the bazaar," I continued, "hopelessly helpless amid the hype." I felt hopelessly helpless in the silence, like a child doing hand puppets for a stoic audience. "That's why we created the Blockchain Investor Scorecard: it's your secret weapon in the Blockchain Bazaar.

"The Blockchain Investor Scorecard was first published in a paper that I coauthored with Harvard economist Navroop Sahdev and Switzerland's own Olga Feldmeier, who organized this great conference today." I led the audience in applause, trying to get a little energy going.

"Our scorecard was adapted from the Timmons Model of Entrepreneurship.[31] The Timmons Model lets you compare very different business opportunities, apples to apples. We just adapted it for the blockchain market.

"We went further than that, by open-sourcing the Blockchain Investor Scorecard. You'll find a copy underneath your chairs." This roused the audience: *free stuff.* "It's quickly becoming the industry standard for rating blockchain investments. Here's how it works." I clicked up the next slide.

Analyzing the Market

	Higher potential (5)	Lower potential (1)	Value
MARKET			
Problem that it solves *Is there a clear problem solved by this token?*	Identified	Unfocused	
Customers *Can you clearly identify who will use this token (job title, demographics, etc.)?*	Reachable and receptive	Unreachable or unlikely to adopt	
Value creation *If a user adopts this token, how much value will be added to his/her business or lifestyle?*	High and identified	None	
Market structure *What is the composition of the market this token will serve?*	Emerging or fragmented	Concentrated or mature	
Market size *Is the potential market too small, too large, or just right?*	$100 million+	<$10 million	

	Higher potential (5)	Lower potential (1)	Value
MARKET			
Regulatory risks *How likely are further regulations on this market, and tokens in general?*	Low	High or highly regulated	
AVERAGE MARKET SCORE *Average the six scores above*			

"*The blockchain is about people*," I emphasized with karate chops. "In order for a blockchain token to have any value, people have to use it. So who will use this blockchain? Not the investor, but the end user? Can we clearly picture this person in our mind? Who is the customer?

"If you were investing in a cousin's sandwich shop, you'd want to know who was going to eat there, how much they'd order, and whether the national demand for sandwiches was growing or shrinking. That's the market. Understand the market for your blockchain investment."

Analyzing Competitive Advantage

	Higher potential (5)	Lower potential (1)	Value
COMPETITIVE ADVANTAGE			
Technology/blockchain platform *Is the token built on a well-known standard blockchain, or is it built from scratch?*	Existing blockchain	New blockchain	
Lead time advantage *Does the team have a head start on companies working on a similar idea?*	Strong	None	
Contacts and networks *What is the team's ability to access key players in this market?*	Well-developed	Limited	
AVERAGE COMPETITIVE ADVANTAGE SCORE *Average the three scores above*			

"Do they have a moat?" I asked. "Something that makes it hard for competitors to storm their castle and overtake them? Do they have some sustainable competitive advantage—a patent, or exclusive partnerships, or a great brand?

ERC-20: a standard for developing blockchain projects on the Ethereum platform. As blockchain standards emerge, they will tend to attract better tools, teams, and talent.

"Take, for example, Ethereum. Created in 2015 by an all-star team of developers, Ethereum is a platform for creating blockchain-based smart contracts. **ERC-20** has quickly become the standard, which means it has better tools, better talent, and better training, and that means it's cheaper and faster to build on Ethereum. Now, that's a mighty moat. Almost a monopoly.

"That said," I continued, "technology moves fast. At one time there was a social networking site called MySpace that looked unassailable. They had one hundred million users.[32] The company was valued at $12 billion.[33] Today, I have to remind you what MySpace was." I paused. "It was a social networking site."

One or two people in the front row chuckled. *Finally.*

Analyzing the Management Team

	Higher potential (5)	Lower potential (1)	Value
MANAGEMENT TEAM			
Entrepreneurial team *Does the team have a demonstrated track record of success?*	All-star "supergroup"	Weak team or solopreneur	
Industry/technical experience *Does the team have "10,000 hours" of experience in this industry?*	Super track record	Newbies	
Integrity *Does the team demonstrate scrupulous honesty and complete transparency?*	Highest standards	Questionable	
AVERAGE MANAGEMENT SCORE *Average the two scores above*			

"THE TEAM." I looked at the slide. "How many venture capitalists do we have in the audience?" A few people raised their hands. "How important is the team?" I called out.

Swiss crickets.

"Maybe *most* important," I stumbled on, "because the team is the one thing you can actually *see*. Does the team have a demonstrated track record of success? Have they worked in this industry? Do they fill you with trust and confidence? Even young teams, fresh out of college, should have accomplishments."

Someone in the back gave me a thumbs-up. Swiss getting loose. Next slide.

Analyzing Token Mechanics

	Higher potential (5)	Lower potential (1)	Value
TOKEN MECHANICS			
Token required *Does the problem truly require a token, or is it a "bolt-on blockchain"?*	Impossible without	Token unnecessary	
Value added *Does the token add a new type of value, or is it "another one of those"?*	Highly differentiated	Copycat token	
Decentralized *Is it truly decentralized (like a mesh network), or is it run by the company (like a cell tower)?*	Users do the work	Company does the work	
Token supply *Is there a known quantity of tokens, or can more be issued in the future, diluting the value?*	Fixed, predictable	Uncertain, inflatable	
Public exchange *On which digital exchanges will the token be listed?*	Known, reputable	Unknown or disreputable	
MVP *Is there an existing product, or a Minimum Viable Product?*	Functioning product	White paper only	
AVERAGE TOKEN SCORE *Average the six scores above*			

"Investing in blockchain tokens is like investing in a mini-economy. Think of it like buying a foreign currency. You want currencies that are going to be strong and stable (like the Swiss franc), not prone to inflation and manipulation (like the Venezuelan bolivar).

"First, is a token even necessary? We see many blockchain projects where the problem would be more easily solved with a centralized database. Blockchain is *de*centralized: no company should own it. Some companies are just riding the hype cycle. Beware the blockchain bandwagon.

"Will the token be listed on a digital exchange? In other words, if you want to sell the token later, will there be a market of buyers and sellers? Or will you be stuck with a token that no one wants, trying to find buyers on Twitter?

"Finally, demand a demo. If they've got a big idea for a blockchain project, make them at least hack together a basic prototype. We call it an MVP: minimum viable product. People are throwing money at blockchain projects based on nothing more than a PowerPoint slide that looks like this."

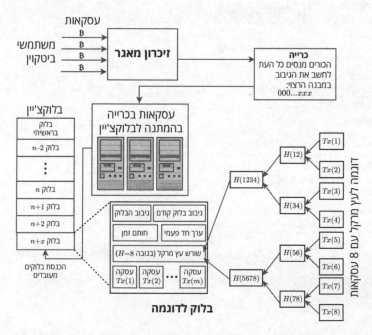

"Bitcoin blockchain–01.png" by Yossiea is licensed under CC BY–SA 4.0.

Here I got a real laugh, because everyone in the room had seen this kind of diagram. Next slide.

Analyzing User Adoption

USER ADOPTION			
Technical difficulty *Will a nontechnical person be able to understand this idea?*	Nontechnical	Highly technical	
Halo Effect *Is the token strongly associated with well-regarded brands or institutions?*	Strong halo effect	Weak or no halo	
Buzz *Are people talking about it? How many followers do they have on social media?*	High social buzz	Low social buzz	
AVERAGE USER ADOPTION SCORE *Average the three scores above*			

"Humans are herd animals," I pronounced. "We're easily fooled by 'cognitive biases' like a good company story, or famous founders, or simply everyone else saying the project is great.[34] Richard Feynman said, 'The first principle is that you must not fool yourself—and you are the easiest person to fool.'[35]

"This presents investors with a dilemma. On the one hand, we must guard against our own cognitive biases. On the other hand, cognitive biases matter. If a blockchain project has a great origin story, founders from Google or Uber, and glowing articles in financial publications, then investors will believe the token is valuable, and it probably *will* go up in price. In that case, why *shouldn't* you invest?"

Something struck me. "*Perception dictates reality.*"

I paused. Where did that come from? And why with such force?

"Perception dictates reality," I continued off-script. "If enough people believe it, it becomes our shared reality. The most unlikely things can happen. Just look at the United States government." Easy laugh.

Averaging the Analysis

OVERALL SCORE		
Weighted average of the five section scores above		

"Those are the five categories of the Blockchain Investor Scorecard," I said, clicking up my final slide. "Then you average them up to get a 1- to 5-star rating. It's like a Yelp rating for blockchain investors.

"Everyone wants to know the future. When will bitcoin hit $20,000 again? When will blockchain take over the world? When will we all become billionaires?

"No one can predict the future of blockchain." I held out my hands. "We can't even predict what Tesla stock will do next week. Elon Musk could slip in the shower, hit his head on the tub, and it's all over. Blockchain is even more volatile than Elon Musk.

"We can't predict the future, but we can predict the present," I concluded. "The Blockchain Investor Scorecard is a powerful weapon for predicting the present. I'm John Hargrave, and I thank you for your presence."

Applause. Applause! Shaky start, but I might have pulled it off. My mind was already presenting a list of improvements: *Tone down the comedy. Lose the bit about the weed token. What were you thinking? Also: upgrade wardrobe.*

The emcee was standing offstage, next to the soundboard. "'Crypto will never last'?" I asked him, shaking my head. "When did I say that?"

He looked confused. "On your blog, mate."

"What are you talking about?"

"Here, I've got it in a tab here." He fiddled with his laptop and passed it over to me. On the screen was a blog post I had written called "This Is Why 'Cryptocurrency' Will Never Last."

"I was talking about the WORD!" I clarified. "I was saying that banks won't adopt a WORD like 'cryptocurrency.' They'll call it something like *digital assets* or *altcoins.*"

"Well, you did say it wouldn't last."

Fortunately, Olga Feldmeier, producer of Crypto Summit and CEO of SMART VALOR, interrupted us. "I took a risk," she said. "I didn't know how you'd do here. The Swiss are very reserved. And . . ."

"And . . ." I repeated, my heart slowing to a crawl.

Here she broke into a smile. "And you made us look good."

My heart started beating again. "Thank you, Olga."

Just then I got a text. It was from Pete.

Big deal on the table.
You won't believe this one.

Then a few seconds later:

How far away is Poland?

CHAPTER 17

The Can Is the Coin

"It's a Polish energy drink company," Pete told me.

"A Polish energy drink company," I repeated stupidly.

"Like Red Bull." Pete nodded. "But Polish."

"Red Pole."

I looked out the window of my hotel room. It was winter in Warsaw, with a sky the color of factory smoke. My body had given up on time zones.

"They really want to move forward on our proposal," Pete said on the satellite window, "but they need to meet you first."

"How much are we talking?" asked Jade, our home office visible behind her.

"At least $25K. More to follow."

"It's agency work, Pete," I sighed.

"We need it," Jade cut in. "Still no payment from Sooyoung. Also . . ." She paused. "We lost another client today." I deflated further.

"Our existing agency clients are asking, 'Do you guys even do agency work anymore?'" Pete said, peering over his glasses. "They go to our website, all they see is blockchain, blockchain, blockchain."

"It's like we're running two companies," said Jade. "The old agency business and the new blockchain business."

"It is a weird time of transition," I admitted. "Hence my meeting today with a Polish energy drink company."

Pete let out a hoot. "We've already presented to their marketing director," he recounted. "Now we just need to pitch to their executive team."

"Who?"

"The founder and the CFO." The big guy and the money guy.

"Do you think they'll give me an energy drink beforehand?" I rubbed my eyes. "I could use one . . . or twelve."

The receptionist *did* offer me a sample, which tasted like Red Bull. It was a sleek white lobby pulsing with excitement, with framed photos of young people enjoying high-energy activities like dancing and crushing homework. Electronica pulsed from white Bose speakers.

"This way." The receptionist ushered me into a drab conference room, where a trio of dour-faced executives were waiting. It was such a stark contrast from the lobby that I was thrown momentarily.

"Hello!" I greeted them, a little too loudly. The energy drink was kicking in.

"John." The marketing director nodded. "Good to meet you in person. This is my assistant, and our CFO, Bartosz."

"A pleasure to meet you all." We shook hands and I pulled out my laptop. "I kicked back a can before I came in, so forgive me if I'm a little wired."

"Yes." She stared at me, stone-faced.

"Speaking of wired," I said, "do you have a cable to your screen here?" This was the ritual before every meeting: spend fifteen minutes trying to get the laptop connected to the screen. The assistant jumped up to help.

"Where's your founder?" I asked politely.

"He is not here," said the marketing director.

"Okay." Silence. "Should we wait for him?"

"He is in Bangkok."

I blinked. *I . . . came to Poland for this.*

"We can make the decision ourselves," Bartosz stated stiffly. I noticed he didn't have a laptop, just a yellow legal pad. He nodded toward the screen, now connected to my laptop. "Please give your presentation."

"BLOCKCHAIN!" I was riding the Polish Bull. "It's the greatest technology of our time! And it is changing the world."

I pulled up a slide that listed hundreds of blockchain projects, grouped by industry. "Blockchain is disrupting finance, health care, education, supply chains, even government. Blockchain is the future.

"I flew here from this blockchain convention"—I clicked to a picture of the convention floor packed wall-to-wall with well-dressed Swiss bankers—"and, boy, are my arms *not* tired. Thanks to your beverage."

Somber silence. I was fighting a cold war.

"Here's the opportunity," I pitched. "*The Official Energy Drink of the Blockchain Revolution.* Imagine giving away your beverage at blockchain conferences around the world. Maybe you make a new flavor. Can you *double the caffeine?*" I shouted.

"We can double the caffeine, yes," the marketing director replied.

"What the hey, triple it!" I clicked to the next slide. "But it gets better. Imagine if every can comes with a coin."

"In the can?" Bartosz asked. "People will choke."

"Not a physical coin," I explained, "a blockchain-based token. Your own digital currency!"

"The can is the cryptocurrency," the marketing director explained to Bartosz.

"The can is the coin! Customers will buy more cans, so they earn more coins. They can buy and sell your coins—your blockchain tokens—on exchanges."

"It's like reward points," the marketing director translated.

"Like reward points that have real-world value!" I was on a roll. "Can you imagine how that would boost sales? Your customers would drink nothing else. Let's patent this!"

"How does this work?" asked Bartosz, confused.

"Imagine a scannable code on the can," I began.

"A QR code," the marketing director helped me. "Like we did for our giveaway."

"Right." I pointed at her. "You buy a can, you scan the code on the can with your phone, it opens an app that awards you one coin. Let's call this idea CaffeineChain." I grabbed my Moleskine notebook and sketched out:

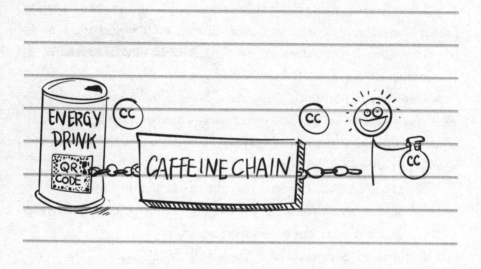

"You're creating these coins—let's call them CaffeineCoins—out of thin air," I explained, "but they have real-world value, because people will be able to redeem them for real-world prizes, like trips and concerts."

The marketing director was nodding. "Like our sweepstakes last year."

"Just think of them like reward points, stored on the blockchain. The difference is that people can buy and sell the rewards points with each other."

"Who determines the value of the rewards points?" asked Bartosz.

"The market!" I exclaimed.

"So five thousand CaffeineCoins earn you one trip," Bartosz reasoned, "and the trip costs us five thousand *złotych*. One CaffeineCoin equals one *złoty*. Now people start trading CaffeineCoins for double the price. One CaffeineCoin now equals two *złotych*. Why would anyone redeem them for the trip?"

"Maybe they start buying CaffeineCoins as an investment!" I smiled confidently.

"Now say they go down to half the value. Or a tenth the value. Let's say you can go buy as many CaffeineCoins as you want and redeem them for prizes—which we have to pay for, with real money."

"But that wouldn't happen," I objected, "as long as they can be redeemed for real-world value. The market will gravitate toward the value of your prizes."

"Hmph." He tapped his pen. "Who oversees all this?"

"That's the best part!" I replied brightly. "It's decentralized! No one owns it!"

"So we have people buying and selling an unregulated security, on an unlicensed exchange, and we are directly liable." He glared at me. "And it is called 'CaffeineCoin.' "

I looked over at the marketing director. No help there.

"It doesn't have to be called CaffeineCoin," I replied, crashing down from my caffeine high. "Look, your founder is totally on board with this idea. He gets it."

"Our founder is in Bangkok," said Bartosz. I glanced at his yellow legal pad. He had written only one word, crossed out:

BLOCKCHAIN

When I got back to my hotel room, I had an email from the energy drink founder waiting for me. I flipped open the videoconference app and gave him a call.

"John? Hey." It was dark on his side, and I could barely make him out. "Sorry I couldn't be there today. I'm in Bangkok."

"I heard."

"How'd it go?"

"Bartosz is a tough sell."

He laughed. "That's why he's in charge of the money."

"What brings you to Bangkok?" I asked. "Business?"

"No, just chilling. Here, let me turn on a light." Suddenly his video window came to life to reveal he wasn't wearing a shirt.

"You know, I'm a serial entrepreneur," he said lazily, a beer in hand. "Started the energy drink company, bought a boatload of bitcoin, now I'm kind of a digital nomad. Right now I'm spending a few months in Thailand." I heard what sounded like an electric bug zapper.

I reflected on my life, which consisted of nonstop work, versus his life, which looked like nonstop leisure. Yet he had the profitable energy drink company, and we were struggling to get payment from our horrible banking client.

"Maybe I should put on some clothes," he laughed, as if seeing my dress shirt and sport coat for the first time.

"I always dress up for videoconferences," I said, "but you do you."

"One second." He left the camera on, and I reflected on what was happening. I came to Warsaw to videoconference with him in Thailand. Off camera, the bug zapper again. Distantly, a rooster crowed.

He came back a few minutes later wearing a white linen shirt left unbuttoned. He was in remarkably good shape, and I briefly worried this videoconference might go somewhere unexpected. "So, we going to do this thing, or what?" he asked.

"Bartosz didn't seem too hot on it," I confessed. "Even though I brought the energy."

"Look, the final decision is mine. It's a great idea. *The Official Energy Drink of the Blockchain Revolution.* The can is the coin. We'll figure out the details as we go along. That's what entrepreneurs do."

"Absolutely."

"Let's do this!" he bellowed.

"Let's do this!" I echoed.

I was elated as I logged off my computer and crawled into bed. We were doing this! But just before I drifted off to sleep, an unwelcome thought jostled its way into my head: *What, exactly, are we doing?*

CHAPTER 18

Unreserved

I didn't understand the word "irony" until the day I found myself in the basement of the Federal Reserve, working on a deal that would replace the Federal Reserve.

Boston's Federal Reserve building is a massive thirty-two-story monolith, not unlike the mysterious structure in Stanley Kubrick's *2001: A Space Odyssey*, only white. Standing in front of this structure is humbling and awe-inspiring, and somehow I had been invited inside. The occasion was a conference on blockchain technology, where an executive from the Federal Reserve gave a surprisingly powerful speech about how blockchain was changing global financial markets. I found it hard to concentrate, because I was fixated on one thought: *I'm inside the freaking Fed.*

The United States Federal Reserve is perhaps the most powerful organization on the planet. It maintains stability of the financial system through a diverse and complicated set of powers: setting interest rates, managing the U.S. Treasury, issuing currency, regulating private banks, and serving as a "lender of last resort." If financial systems are built on trust, the Fed might be the most trusted institution in the world.

The Federal Reserve is a bank, but it's also a building—twelve buildings, to be exact. And I was sitting in the basement of the Boston branch, in the belly of the beast: the lunchroom.

"We're launching a new **stablecoin**," our prospective client was explaining via videoconference.

"What's that?" Pete asked.

"Stablecoins," repeated the prospect, a fast-talking former currency trader who had gone full-time into blockchain. "Like bitcoin but stable. Pegged to the U.S. dollar."

"So you buy one of these stablecoins," I clarified, "and it holds its value?"

"Right. One of our coins is worth one dollar. It won't fluctuate like bitcoin. Have you seen the price today?"

Stablecoin: an altcoin that is pegged to a stable asset, such as the U.S. dollar. Stablecoins provide an easy way to "hold value" in digital currencies, without having to constantly convert back to dollars.

KEY TERM

"Don't remind me," I groaned.

"Can you imagine what it's like to trade this stuff?" he went on. "Where do you park your money at night? You close out all your positions, transfer it all to bitcoin so you can get some sleep, you wake up the next morning, *boom!* Lost half its value."

In my Moleskine notebook, I wrote:

STABLECOINS =
A PLACE TO PARK MONEY

"So your stablecoin is always worth a dollar," Pete clarified.

"Right. Backed by gold. If you buy a dollar of our token, we have it backed by a dollar's worth of gold."

"Where is the gold?" I asked.

"In a vault."

"Where is the vault?"

He laughed evasively. "Somewhere safe. Investors will be able to verify the gold in the vault, through a real-time camera, and numbered gold bars that will also be tracked on the blockchain."

"At this moment," I bragged, "I am surrounded by enormous vaults holding millions of dollars in U.S. currency. I am literally surrounded by money."

"But that money has no intrinsic value," he shot back. "Not since Nixon took the U.S. off the gold standard in 1971."

"Now you have a digital currency," I responded, "which many believe has no intrinsic value, that's once again backed by actual gold."

Pete howled. "I can't believe you're in the commissary of the Fed!"

"Sadly, a bowl of soup is $100 trillion," I said.

"We've got to get the word out about our stablecoin," our prospect continued, ignoring me. "Can you help us put together a marketing plan?"

"You've got to do more than that," I told him. "You've got to build trust. Why should investors trust that you really have the gold in your vault?"

"Because they'll be able to see a time-stamped—"

"Hollywood magic," I objected, waving him away. "Moon landing."

"But the numbered gold bars—"

"Front-screen projection," I cut him off.

"The audit trail on the blockchain—"

"We are not rational creatures. If we want to believe in something, we'll believe in it to our dying breath. If we don't want to believe in it, no amount of logic will convince us otherwise."

"Hmm." This got through to him. "So how do you get people to believe in it?"

"Trust."

"How do you build trust?"

This was a new question. In fact, it seemed to be the central question. Posed in the central bank!

"Reputation helps," Pete offered. "You do a lot of good work over a long period of time. Reputation and reliability."

"I guess it's like trusting a person," I added. "Trust takes time."

"What did Warren Buffett say?" asked our prospect. "'It takes twenty years to build trust, and five minutes to destroy it.' Something like that."[36]

"Your twenty years starts now." I smiled. "Shall we get started?"

"Yes," he replied impatiently. "Let's go."

"I'll get the agreement set up for you," said Pete, but the rest was cut off by a large security guard standing at my table.

"You're going to have to turn off the webcam," said the guard. He wasn't messing around: he didn't say "sir."

"Gotta go, fellas," I told them, signing off.

I packed up my laptop and made my way back through the security gates, metal detectors, and armed guards, where I enjoyed a final gaze at the enormous gold seal of the Federal Reserve: the mighty eagle, its wings outstretched. Now that I looked more closely, it kind of looked like a mascot in a bird suit.

I stepped out into the cold sunshine of Boston's Blockchain District, reflecting on Yuval Noah Harari's ideas about money. "Trust is the raw material from which all types of money are minted . . . ," he wrote in *Sapiens: A Brief History of Mankind*. To which he added: "*money is the most universal and most efficient system of mutual trust ever devised*."[37]

Again I was struck with an ironic thought. Everyone was talking about digital currencies replacing the dollar, so why were we creating "stablecoins" that were now pegged to the dollar? It was like declaring you're going to start your own country, but only after getting permission from your existing country.

Getting permission before declaring independence? That's kind of not how we do it in the U.S.

That was the ticking time bomb that lodged in my brain, and now I've placed it in yours. The very ideals of the United States could be turned back against itself.

From the earliest age I was taught that the United States fought a valiant war for independence from its tyrannical British overlords. But if that spirit of independence was really embedded in our national DNA, why shouldn't that independence be wielded against the United States itself?

"Is independence really a U.S. value?" I asked aloud as I walked by the Boston Tea Party Museum. "Isn't it a *human* value? And isn't this human thirst for independence a higher authority than a government?" I stopped in my tracks. "In our quest for independence, *why do we need to ask for permission?*"

This was the kind of thinking that would surely lead to trouble.

CHAPTER 19

Ladies First

The idea was simple: *Shark Tank* for blockchain.

Also, the judges would all be women.

You're probably familiar with the reality show *Shark Tank* (also known as *Dragons' Den*). An aspiring entrepreneur pitches his or her idea to a panel of successful investors, who try to find weaknesses in the business plan. Then the panelists either pass on the offer or invest on the spot.

The drama is watching the entrepreneurs squirm as the sharks put them through their paces. *What a perfect idea for blockchain*, I thought. We could teach investors how to think about new blockchain projects, educating while entertaining. A blockchain *Shark Tank* seemed inevitable.

Now here we were, with another sold-out blockchain event at TechLab. We had cameras and lights; we had even hired a musician to warm up the crowd. This was not just another boring blockchain panel; this was a *show*! It was coming together, people!

"How many ladies in the house?" I asked the crowd, and a chorus of hoots and hollers went up. "As you ladies know, blockchain is bro-heavy. That is why we need more women to get involved, to make your voices heard. Tonight, you are making your voices heard." Cheers. One woman was wearing a T-shirt that read SATOSHI IS FEMALE.

"Lot of dudes in blockchain," I riffed. "Too much testosterone can be dangerous. It leads to crazy, risk-taking behaviors, like getting involved with blockchain." Pause for laughs. "We need strong, smart women to bring a different perspective. We have three of the strongest and smartest here tonight.

"Ladies and gentlemen—but mostly ladies—please welcome Jessica, Navroop, and Diane!" Our musician, recording artist Jodi Heights, played a theme song as the judges entered to big applause.

"And our three blockchain entrepreneurs: Jay, Mac, and Andrew!" Another music sting, more applause. We needed spotlights. And a set. And sponsors. These events were costing us a fortune.

The format worked even better than I had imagined. Each entrepreneur had five minutes to pitch his idea, and the women would grill him. They were all supersmart and savvy, and as I listened to the entrepreneurs wrestle with the sharks, I was glad that I was just the host.

"You say you're looking to raise $10 million," asked Jessica, an IBM executive. "What will you do with that money?"

"First, product development," responded Jay, who was building a platform to track social media activity around various altcoins. "Then marketing. Then . . ." he trailed off.

"I'm going to pass on this one," Jessica concluded.

"How will you get people to use your product?" asked Navroop, a research fellow at MIT. "How will your blockchain achieve critical mass?"

"Word of mouth," said Mac, who was building a blockchain platform for trading favors. "The nature of the platform is that it will grow organically, people helping people. Right?"

"You tell me!" Navroop shot back.

"Who else is on your team?" asked Diane, a work-from-home mom and blockchain investor. "What else have they done?"

"Just me and my cofounder," admitted Andrew, who was leading a blockchain development company. "But we have a large network of pro-grammers around the world."

"How many? Where are they? How much blockchain experience?"

It was uncomfortably wonderful.

As a bonus, we handed out Blockchain Investor Scorecards, so the au-dience could rate each project themselves. After a round of audience ques-tions, we ushered each entrepreneur into the Cone of Silence and took a vote: How many people would personally invest in this blockchain token?

This experience was invaluable, because it allowed us to see how blockchain investors actually *thought*. What questions did they ask? How did they make decisions? The women on our panel modeled the kind of laser drilling that investors should do before putting in their hard-earned money.

"Don't be afraid to ask questions," I told the crowd. "And please don't ever start by saying, 'This may be a stupid question.' It's *never* a stupid question. You're just giving away your own power, telling the world you're stupid. If you have the question, someone else does, too. *Just ask the question.*

"Why do we give away our power?" I asked, with no idea where I was going with this. "We can claim our power." I stopped.

What in God's name did any of this have to do with blockchain? I had the sensation of a cartoon character who runs out over a cliff, then realizes he's hanging in midair. It was a sensation that I would come to know well.

"We can claim our power," I repeated. I looked over at Jodi to save me. She nodded.

"We can claim our power," I concluded. "Jodi Heights!"

With her shock of pink-and-violet hair, Jodi looked elegant as she sat down at the keyboard and began to sing.

What is the meaning of this?
Don't feed me empty words.

So I want to be more than just a pretty face.
There are things I was born to do.
I will never make history by always behaving like a lady.

My eyes moistened. There was so much *heart* in this. It went so far beyond the technology! Blockchain was just the vessel that we were using to bring this message out into the world. I looked at the audience to see if they were feeling it. A few women were wiping away tears.

An image came to mind. Each morning during my meditation practice, I pictured a golden light surrounding my heart, slowly growing to surround my body, then my family and home, then my local community, then Boston, then the United States, then the Earth.

Now this visual sprang to mind unbidden: that pure golden light bursting forth from my heart, spreading throughout this event room at TechLab, flowing into the hearts of everyone there, nourishing and recharging, then flowing back to me, magnified in purity and intensity.

"We will never make history by always behaving like a lady," I said, repeating the last line of Jodi's song. "Let's make history together. Big round of applause for Jodi Heights!" Which we got.

As I was leaving TechLab a few hours later, Benedict was waiting at the front desk. "John." He flashed that airport-runway smile.

"Hey, Benedict." My hands were full of equipment. "Thanks for your help tonight."

"I'm glad the event went well," he said, "but some of my staff say you were disrespectful to the women."

"I was—what?" I dropped my bags in surprise.

"You yelled at Yolanda before the event."

I pinched the bridge of my nose. "The room wasn't ready," I explained. "She was supposed to have it clean, right?"

"We had a big event earlier today. That room gets a lot of use."

"That room was a disaster. Garbage all over the place. Leftover pizza boxes. My team was trying to get this event ready. I may have been a little short-tempered. I'm sorry."

"You've got to treat women as equals," he said.

"Are you—" I looked closely to see if he was joking. He wasn't. "Do you know what this event was all about?"

"Blockchain, right? Look, I'll smooth things over with Yolanda. But, seriously, you've got to get people out of here quicker after these events."

"You do know this is free publicity for TechLab, right?" I asked.

"But we've got to stay afterward to clean up."

"You and Yolanda?" I asked. "Because cleaning is not her strong suit."

For the first time his smile wavered. "Yes," he replied. "Me and Yolanda."

"Good luck," I said, picking up my bags and storming out.

Looking back, this was probably the straw that broke Benedict's back.

CHAPTER 20

At the Corner of Blockchain and Mania

"Hey, guys!" I yelled. "Can you keep it down? I've got to take this interview!"

"Sorry," said Nick, turning down Lady Gaga's "Born This Way." We were weaving through Boston traffic, trying to make it to our 9:00 a.m. event to kick off Boston Blockchain Week. We had rented a bus and turned it into a party on six wheels: *the Blockchain Bus*.

I flicked on my wireless headset. "This is John."

"John? Steve from National Public Radio. This still a good time?"

"As good a time as any." I looked around at the wide assortment of freaks and geeks on the Blockchain Bus. We had removed the seats and hung a disco ball. There was a lavish breakfast spread, and a few people were getting the drinking started early. Outside the bus, it was rush hour on a Monday.

"Great," Steve responded. "Let me just start the recording."

"Take your time." I looked out the window, where some guy was furiously honking, trying to get around us. The bus was jammed between lanes, and it soon turned into a cacophony of honks. The Blockchain Bus was the Block-Traffic Bus.

Apparently none of this madness was making it through my headset. "So I'll ask you a few questions," Steve continued, "and we'll edit it down to about ten seconds to run during NPR drive time. First off, tell us about Boston Blockchain Week."

"In ten seconds?" I clarified.

"Or less."

"It's a weeklong series of events put on by the Boston blockchain community. You know, the blockchain is decentralized, and so is Boston Blockchain Week. No one owns it. Everyone contributes."

"Got it. And could you also just quickly explain what blockchain is?"

"*In ten seconds?*"

He laughed. "Or less."

"No. No, I cannot."

"Please try."

"Open-source data. Like open-source software. Bitcoin is open-source money; blockchain is open-source data."

"Expand on that a little."

"In ten seconds."

He laughed. "Right."

"Just think about blocks and chains. Every time the two of us exchange money, we write down the transaction on a block of wood. Then we connect those blocks using a chain, so we can see the sequence of transactions. Then we put it in a public space, so everyone can see it and add to it."

"That's what you mean by 'open-source.'"

"That's blockchain."

Blocks and Chains

My friend Jim, a fellow geek who also happens to be handy with tools, actually did this. He cut a bunch of wood blocks, personalized each one for a friend or family member, then strung them together with chains.

He was kind of doing it as a goof, making fun of the hype around blockchain—but before long, the project went viral and he had hundreds of people sending him money to personalize their blocks on the Literal Blockchain, in the same way that people will buy a memorial brick at the local playground.

He donated the money to charity. He did not use it to start his own blockchain lumber company.

To visualize blockchain systems, this concept of "blocks" and "chains" is helpful. The blockchain isn't a physical "thing," but sometimes you need to draw it like one.

For example, let's take a hypothetical blockchain project called "DriveChain," designed to hold all your driving data: when you left the house, when you arrived, how many miles you drove, how fast you were traveling, and so on. Let's say you have a little GPS device that tracks all this data automatically.

This is valuable information. An auto insurance company can use it, for example, to develop personalized rates for you. (A safe, infrequent driver will get better rates than a reckless, frequent one.)

The insurance company can store all this data in huge centralized databases, which is exactly how they operate today. But they could also store this data in a blockchain, which we can show like this:

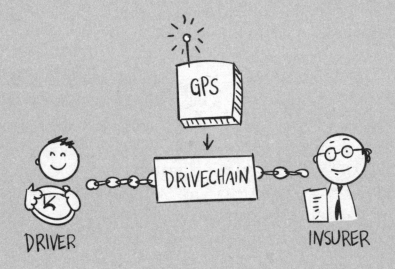

The "block" represents the blockchain itself (i.e., the distributed ledger), with the users of that ledger represented on both sides. Remember the ledger is *distributed*, meaning it's replicated across hundreds or thousands of different computers. (No one person owns it.) But, for simplicity, let's draw it as a block.

Because a blockchain is often a two-sided marketplace—bitcoin, for example, has a "buyer" and a "seller"—we connect the two parties to the block with a chain. And the GPS unit, which is just feeding the blockchain with data on your driving behavior, is shown with an arrow.

What we've done with this simple diagram is profound: now the data no longer sits on some insurance company's computer. It's now on a shared blockchain that *multiple* insurance companies can access, all competing to give each driver the best rates, based on his or her risk profile.

Geico's famous tagline is "Fifteen minutes could save you 15 percent or more on car insurance." By giving better information to insurers, blockchain could save us a lot more than that.

We got to our location just before 9:00 a.m., delighted to find a small crowd assembled so early on a Monday. The media were hungry for anything about blockchain, especially a press conference as weird as this one.

I climbed onto the very top of a ladder that was set up there—stepping onto the warning label that read DO NOT STAND ON THIS STEP—and held on to the street sign so I wouldn't fall off.

"*Beacon Street!*" I began. "The birthplace of American history." From my perch atop the ladder, a gust of wind hit me, and I wobbled a bit, tightening my grip on the Beacon Street sign.

"Just down this street"—I waved carefully with my free hand—"is the Granary Burying Ground, the resting place of great patriots like John Hancock, Samuel Adams, and Paul Revere. Just up this way is the Massachusetts State House, the seat of our government. It is the street that started a nation!"

A police car drove by slowly, and I watched it with trepidation. We didn't exactly have permission to be doing this.

"Beacon Street is the birthplace of American history. How fitting that it is also the birthplace of Boston's blockchain scene. Which is why today we are *renaming Beacon Street . . .*"

Wendy from our Media Shower team handed me the new street sign. It looked amazing.

"*. . . to Blockchain Street!*"

The street sign was flawless. I don't know how Wendy got it done—the stamped green metal, the clean white lettering—and when I held it up to the original sign, it fit perfectly.

The crowd cheered as we placed our new sign on top of the old one. We had prepped it with Velcro so it would be easy to remove. I looked around for the police officer. So far, so good.

"Three cheers for blockchain!" I shouted, raising my fist. "Hip hip, hooray!" I punched the air. "Hip, hip, *hooray!*" Another punch. "Hip, hip, *hoo*RAGHH!" My ladder gave way, and I frantically grabbed the street sign, dangling eight feet above the sidewalk.

Before the fall.

"Can you believe that media coverage today?" Pete laughed later that night. We were once again packed inside the Blockchain Bus, and the dance floor was jumping—quite literally, because occasionally the bus would hit a pothole.

"I haven't had this much fun since the dot-com days!" I replied, shouting to be heard over the disco music.

"This is *awesome*," Pete agreed. "Everyone wants exposure! We've got so many deals on the table."

"We are actually turning this into a blockchain media company!"

Pete raised his beer and toasted my shot glass, which was filled with milk. We kicked them back.

"We've arrived!" I yelled.

"Yeah, things are going pretty good."

"No, I mean we've *arrived*!" I pointed out the window.

"This stop," the DJ smoothly announced over the sound system, "is the historic *Blockchain Street* sign. You've read about it; you've seen it on TV. Christened just this morning, the historic *Blockchain Street* sign." Laughing, we spilled out of the bus to admire our handiwork.

The sign was gone.

Not just our Blockchain Street sign, which was just Velcroed on: the *entire street sign* was missing. Like someone stole history. No more Blockchain Street. No more Beacon Street!

"Did someone steal it?" Pete wondered. "As a souvenir?"

I was speechless. What did this mean?

"All right!" I said, ushering everyone back into the bus. "Nothing to see here! Like, literally, there is *nothing to see here*."

Our DJ started up the tunes, the bus driver closed the doors, and soon we were on our way again. Pete and I rode in silence for a while, each lost in thought.

"Maybe we should have asked permission," I admitted.

Pete chuckled. "Probably just some kids took it," he concluded. "Want another shot?" He jiggled the milk jug.

I looked at the milk with distaste; the evening had been spoiled.

"Your next party," shouted the bus driver, throwing open the doors, "brought to you by Pillar VC, building the next generation of blockchain tech companies!" Out poured the crowd of rowdy revelers, draining into the club. Pete and I followed, but something stopped me.

"I'll be there in a minute," I told Pete, motioning for him to go inside. I had spotted an old friend outside the party casually chatting with another investor.

"Martin?" I timidly interrupted their conversation as I approached.

"John!" He seemed genuinely glad to see me. His frizz blew lightly in the breeze as if waving hello.

I introduced myself to his companion, another angel investor in the Boston tech scene. "Martin, I'll call you next week," he said, taking his key from the valet. "Good to meet you, John." He got in his Tesla and drove off.

"This yours?" asked Martin, raising his eyebrows. He nodded toward the bus, emblazoned with a giant *Bitcoin Market Journal* logo.

"Gotta zig when everyone else is zagging." I smiled.

"With the hype around blockchain," he said, "seems to me you're zigging when everyone else is zigging." His frizz bobbed up and down as if nodding in agreement.

"I'm reinventing, Martin. That was your advice. 'Hockey stick growth,' remember?" I pulled out the air quotes. "'What got you here won't get you there.'"

"That does sound like me," he admitted.

"And I'm *finding* it, Martin!" I exclaimed. Maybe it was the milk talking. "I'm getting good at this."

"What is 'this,' exactly?" He punctuated the word with his finger. "Driving a bus?"

"No, it's . . ." I struggled to explain it. "Making blockchain interesting. Easy to understand. Easy to use. Easy to invest."

"And is there money in that?"

"There is a *fire hose* of money," I replied confidently. "I've never seen anything like it."

"And what's the price of bitcoin today?"

"About $8,800."

Martin whistled. "From $20,000 to $8,800 in, what, four months?"

"It's a roller coaster," I admitted. "The highs are really high and the lows are really low."

"And you still don't think it's a bubble?"

"Blockchain is the future. I bet my company on it."

He gave me a hard look. "That's what worries me."

SUMMARY

Let's wrap up the lessons in Part 2 so you can be ready to ride the roller coaster of Part 3.

✦ **The future is unpredictable.** As with any new technology, we can't be sure where blockchain is headed. (Who could have looked at the early Internet and predicted Netflix?)

✦ **Reinventing industries.** That said, blockchain is likely to rewrite the rules for many industries:

  ✦ **Banking:** making it easier to send and receive money

  ✦ **Supply chain:** providing better tracking of raw materials and inventory

  ✦ **Legal:** replacing traditional contracts with software-based smart contracts

  ✦ **Insurance:** providing better rates through better risk profiles

  ✦ **Real estate:** creating new structures of shared ownership

✦ **Energy:** creating blockchain-based marketplaces to buy and sell power

✦ **Internet:** letting our smart devices openly communicate with each other

✦ **Health care:** sharing medical research and health data

✦ **Government:** changing the way we vote

✦ **Finance:** changing the way we invest

✦ **Smart stocks.** Blockchain is improving the world of investing and fund-raising by making tokens that function like a traditional stock, but smarter.

✦ **New financial instruments.** Blockchain will allow us to invest in anything that has value (just as the "Bowie Bond" allowed us to invest in David Bowie's music catalog).

✦ **Do your homework.** Rather than investing on hearsay or emotion, we can use tools like our Blockchain Investor Scorecard to rate and review new blockchain investments. (See **Reference Guide 2**.)

✦ **The Three D's.** Blockchain is decentralized, distributed, and democratic. Like the Internet, no one "owns" it—yet we all do. Beware of tightly controlled private blockchains. Ask yourself: *Why?*

✦ **Blocks and chains.** Don't settle for convoluted descriptions of blockchain that you don't understand. Ask questions until you can draw it in a simple diagram.

✦ **Build trust.** All money is built on trust. Trust takes time.

PART 3

THE FALL

CHAPTER 21

Moody McMarketson

The worst part was not that I was speaking at a Rotary Club for free. The worst part was that I was getting heckled.

My inbox was now flooded with invitations to speak. I accepted all of them. I was constantly working on new material, and I welcomed the chance to practice. I would often record my talks, then watch them afterward, nipping and tucking. In comedy lingo, I was working on my "tight ten."

And today, just like a stand-up comic, I had a heckler.

"You think blockchain will replace *religion*?" asked the gray-haired gentleman sitting at the front table. I was in the function room of an Italian restaurant on Cape Cod, speaking to a crowd of about thirty Rotarians. The mood had been fun-loving and jovial, until he interrupted me.

"I probably wasn't clear," I replied, realizing I had stepped in it. I pointed to the projector screen, titled "Centralization vs. Decentralization." "I was saying that most of the human institutions we've created have been *centralized* institutions. Governments. Corporations. The Church."

"You said the *Catholic* Church," he shot back.

"I did say the Catholic Church," I replied, wishing for a time machine.

"Humans *need* centralized institutions," he argued. "Governments, companies, religions—you think we're going to just throw it all away? That's called anarchy."

"Not if it's recorded on the decentralized ledger . . ." I began.

"What does that even *mean*?" He was really worked up. "My son bought bitcoin when it was $15,000. Today it's half that! Do you know how much money he lost?"

"It's volatile," I agreed. "Like the atmosphere in this room." A few nervous chuckles.

"Look, I don't want to interrupt," he interrupted, "but do you own bitcoin?"

"Yes."

"So you're hawking your own investment! Maybe you just made a bad decision and you should just eat it instead of trying to get everyone else here to eat it with you."

This really stung. I had begun to notice a subculture of "blockchain evangelists," people like me who traveled the world—at their own expense—to preach the virtues of blockchain. Were we really prophets, or were we pitchmen?

"First, I'm a Christian," I said. That threw everyone off balance. "I believe in the Church. We need institutions that help us build community, to nurture our higher values, to help us become our best selves . . ."

"I don't mean to interrupt, but I came to hear about blockchain, to understand why my son bought into this thing, and now you're talking about religion."

Behind the elderly heckler, directly in my line of sight, hung a banner on the wall:

THE ROTARY FOUR-WAY TEST

Of the things we think, say, or do

1. Is it the TRUTH?

2. Is it FAIR to all concerned?

3. Will it build GOODWILL and BETTER FRIENDSHIPS?

4. Will it be BENEFICIAL to all concerned?[38]

"Why has bitcoin lost its value?" I flipped ahead a few slides. "That is a good question. It's the perfect time to introduce our friend, Moody McMarketson."

Mister Market as a Teenager

At the beginning of 2018, people were buying and selling a single bitcoin for $20,000.

In June 2018, just six months later, bitcoin was trading at $7,000. Guess what? *Same bitcoin.*

Nothing changed. If anything, there was more investment and more intelligence pouring into the blockchain industry. So the value of the overall market, in theory, was even higher.

The legendary investor Benjamin Graham had a funny analogy for this, which I'll update for modern times. Imagine the market is a hormonal teenager called Moody McMarketson. Some days Moody is on top of the world. "I'll give you $20,000 for a single bitcoin!" shouts Moody. "I just asked Jenny out to the prom and she said yes! Twenty grand for a bitcoin! Let's do this!"

Other days Moody is down in the dumps. "Jenny stood me

up," he says, slumping onto your couch. He smells of Mountain Dew and Fritos. "I'll sell you back that bitcoin for $7,000." Then he breaks down weeping.

Graham taught that intelligent investors don't have to respond to any of these moods. We can calmly watch as Moody McMarketson goes through the emotional turbulence of adolescence. Tomorrow he'll be back with a new price. And the day after that. We don't have to take any of his offers. We can wait.

Moody McMarketson's prefrontal cortex has not fully evolved, so some of his offers are just downright nuts. When they get unreasonably low, we buy. And when they get unreasonably high, we sell.

"I don't want to interrupt, but I know all about Mr. Market," said my Rotarian rival. "What does this have to do with blockchain?"

"Getting there." I clicked to my next slide.

In the blockchain world, Moody is even moodier. The highs are stratospheric, and the lows are cataclysmic. But what's low and what's high? That's where our investor judgment, informed by careful research and analysis, must override Moody's moods.

To beat the market, you must sometimes bet against the market. This is common sense. You've got to zig when everyone else is zagging and zag when everyone else is zigging. You've got to ignore the market's moods.

It's easy to talk yourself into buying bitcoin when the price is rocketing upward and approaching $20,000. It's not so easy when it's in a prolonged slump at $7,000. But that is exactly what Ben Graham taught: intelligent investors look for great bargains and buy them when they're not fashionable.

Look for blockchain investments on sale.

I can't tell you whether bitcoin is a great value at $7,000, or $2,000, or $200. It's too new. But I can tell you that a $7,000 bitcoin is just a $20,000 bitcoin sitting on a store shelf with a giant red tag saying, *65% OFF.*

Eventually we'll get Moody on medication (Meddy?). The blockchain market will eventually grow up, but markets will always be moody. It's their nature.

As a blockchain investor, be patient. Do your homework. When your careful analysis shows you that the market is undervaluing a token, buy. This is the opposite of what the market will be doing, and that's how fortunes are made.

"I hate to interrupt," my tormentor taunted, "but *blockchains are not companies*. They don't have revenues, expenses, or executives. They don't own physical assets like factories or merchandise. They don't have any of the traditional metrics you would use to evaluate a company's stock."

"Maybe they're more like precious metals," cut in another Rotarian, a heavyset gentleman sitting near the back, "like investing in gold."

"Or commodities," offered a well-dressed woman. "Or foreign currencies."

"All these points of view have benefits and drawbacks," I replied, "but it's most helpful to think of blockchain as its own asset class. *It's something new.*"

I paused, waiting for an interruption. Finally there was silence.

"Value investors look at a company's numbers—corporate earnings, debt levels, net assets, and so on—to determine whether a stock is over-priced or 'on sale.' These metrics measure the health of a company, like a doctor measures your vital signs.

"The blockchain is a different animal. Maybe we can still measure its temperature and its heart rate, but maybe we need new vital signs. Maybe we need new numbers."

I looked at the stack of Blockchain Investor Scorecards I had brought with me. "These are qualitative numbers," I said, holding them up, "but we need *quantitative* numbers. These are opinions, but we need *facts*. A doctor's opinion is important for future health, but vital signs tell us your health now."

There were a fair number of seniors in the room, so maybe the talk of doctors was getting us back on course.

"It's like your banner here." I walked my microphone to the back of the room. "Is it the *truth*? Is it *fair*? Will it build *goodwill*? Will it be *beneficial*? Those are the things we want to find in a smart investment." I paused. "We need new numbers."

"Such as?" needled my nemesis.

"I know: you don't mean to interrupt," I said, and finally drew a laugh.

"You said we need new numbers," he replied, still not smiling. "What are the new numbers?"

"We're working on it."

We *were* working on it. We desperately wanted to value blockchains, to find the one rule that would rule them all.

But in the meantime, we were running out of money. And the market was growing even moodier.

CHAPTER 22

We the People

"And we're live in five . . . four . . . three . . ." Rob paused and pointed at me.

"Welcome to our first *Bitcoin Market Journal* webcast!" I exclaimed brightly, squinting under the hot glow of studio lights. It felt like I was performing for a laptop, but I knew we had a massive audience tuned in to our premiere broadcast.

"We have a very special guest with us today, the man who is putting voting on the blockchain: Mr. Nimit Sawhney, the cofounder and CEO of Voatz!" Off camera, Rob and Wendy applauded from behind their laptops.

Our in-person investor meetings had grown so quickly that they were now standing room only. With the tension simmering between me and Benedict, we decided to offer them as online webinars, which would be easier to stage and attract an even bigger audience. We were going global!

"Nimit," I began, "I read that you grew up in India during the eighties, when the prime minister was assassinated. In the political aftermath, you saw people forced to vote at gunpoint. That image really stuck with

you. So how did you get from there to a blockchain-based voting platform?"[39]

Nimit was a tall, bearded entrepreneur who looked the part of a
humble tech genius. "In 2014 my brother and I were just starting to
learn about blockchain." He was so soft-spoken that I had a hard time
hearing him. "When we took a look at the underlying tech, we were,
like, 'Wow, this is very powerful. You can use it to secure any kind of
digital data.' Elections and voting data seemed like a good fit."

I snuck a glance at the laptop screen, where I saw that Nimit was
several inches taller than me. I looked like a Munchkin. *Why are we
standing? And why don't we have microphones?*

"On a whim," Nimit continued, "we went to the South by South-
west technology festival in Austin, Texas. One day it was raining, and we
walked into this convention room, and a hackathon was happening. It
was completely unplanned.

"So we built this blockchain prototype focused on one particular use
case: how to detect and prevent voter coercion when people vote from
home. We ended up winning first prize and it kick-started our company.
Since then, it's blossomed into a full-fledged elections platform which
uses smartphones and biometrics, then records the votes on the blockchain."

"And it's being used in real elections," I pointed out. "You've handled
more than seventy-five thousand votes across thirty test elections." I
looked at the camera and addressed the multitudes. "If you're new to
blockchain, let me explain how a blockchain-based voting system might
work."

The Transparent Election

Imagine a democracy where every vote is recorded on a block-chain. (Let's call it VoterChain.) You simply open the VoterChain app on your phone, verify your ID, then cast your vote. Your vote is anonymous (I can't see what you voted) but auditable (I can see what everyone voted in total).

This means that third parties can now audit the results of the blockchain and tally the votes themselves. Isn't that the way it should be? VoterChain offers checks and balances: a voting system of the people, for the people, and *owned by* the people.

Forward-thinking governments will create open-source block-chain systems to make every vote transparent. But if you don't live in a forward-thinking nation, here's the most radical idea: you don't need the government's permission to make this work.

Imagine if, on Election Day, citizens hold their own *parallel election* using VoterChain. Two elections: one official but opaque, one unofficial but transparent. Do the two elections agree?

Dishonest elections are nothing new. During the 2016 presidential election in the Democratic Republic of the Congo, the government cut Internet and cell phone service, and banned the use of motor vehicles.[40] Imagine if voters were later able to use VoterChain to show what they would have voted. What would they find?

In Venezuela, citizens have grown so frustrated by the direction under President Nicolás Maduro that they organized mass protests, demanding his resignation—protests that left ninety citizens dead in 2017.[41] Imagine if VoterChain was open for the world to see what Venezuela really wanted. What would we discover?

A project like VoterChain will need to fairly represent all political parties, all the people. But by offering a decentralized alternative to centralized elections, it can truly represent the will of the people.

It's unlikely that corrupt governments will go for this, but we don't need them to make this work. We can opt out of their two-party systems, their toxic political rhetoric. The people can answer to a higher calling than their government: we can answer to our conscience.

"Is this possible?" I asked. "Can you run a parallel election on the blockchain?"

"It's possible, but one thing we would strongly encourage is to get buy-in from all sides of the political spectrum," Nimit replied. I sensed that he was choosing his words carefully. "People have tried this idea in South America, and it gets really partisan really quickly. So that defeats the noble objectives you are trying to achieve. Get all the stakeholders on board, even your election officials."

I realized that Nimit's technology was inherently political. To succeed, platforms like Voatz have to get election officials on board. They do this through small tests—absentee ballots, town votes, polling on citizen issues—work out the kinks, get people used to voting via app. Then blockchain goes big time.

Evolution, not revolution.

Problem was, I wanted it to happen *now*. We all did! Millions of people would soon be watching this video. I pictured them pouring into Washington, D.C., marching in Parliament Square, holding hands in Caracas and Harare and Pyongyang. All chanting, "We the people! WE the people! *WE THE PEOPLE!*"

"That was truly inspiring," I told the team on our debrief call a few minutes later. Nimit had just left the building, and I was still riding high. "Rob, how many viewers?"

"Well," Rob said from behind his laptop. "At our peak, we had almost twenty-five people."

The smile was frozen on my face. "And how many of those were Media Shower employees?"

"About half."

I blinked. "But we had so many sign-ups for this webinar."

"Bitcoin price is wavering around $7,000," Jade suggested from our home office. "That has an impact."

"So the whole blockchain market rides on the price of bitcoin?!"

"Maybe it all moves in parallel," she suggested. "Like the stock market."

The camera lights were still blazing, and I turned them off, temporarily stunned. Just then, Benedict knocked on the door of the conference room. "Can I see you a minute?" he asked.

I followed him out into the hallway, where he flashed me that smile. "Hey, I have to ask you guys to take down all the video equipment."

"We booked the conference room," I shot back, annoyed.

"Yeah, but you're not allowed to film inside the building without permission. You were supposed to submit a request."

I gritted my teeth. "Next time we'll submit a request."

"There won't be a next time." He smiled. "No more filming. Period."

"Benedict"—I took a deep breath—"you're being unreasonable."

"You don't ask for permission after the fact," he stated. "Pack it up."

In the space of an hour, we had gone from evolution to ejection. I entered the conference room, thoroughly defeated. "The revolution will not be televised," I told the team. "Pack it up."

Evolution or revolution? The question weighed heavily on my mind, because tomorrow I would be meeting with the U.S. government.

CHAPTER 23

Empowering the 99 Percent

The government conference room was brown: walls, chairs, table, cabinets. As the government officials shook hands with us, even their suits were brown.

Increasingly, we had been invited to speak to government committees, politicians running for office, even ambassadors from other countries. They liked that we were able to explain blockchain simply; they needed to know what to do about it.

But today was a big one. Today we were talking with the regulators! If meeting with the head of the SEC was like an audience with the pope, this would be like meeting the pope's top cardinals—if the cardinals wore corduroy.

As we took our seats around the conference table—*Government on one side*, I noted, *us on the other*—I reflected on how different the tech startup culture was from the people who regulated it. A pitcher of ice water sat in one corner, whereas at TechLab we had a case of Polish energy drinks.

"Welcome," said the presiding government official to our little crew of blockchain leaders. "The purpose of our fact-finding meeting today is to *gather information*. We're just trying to see what's going on in the blockchain space. We've asked each of you to say a few words. Who would like to begin?"

"I'll go," I offered, and no one was surprised.

"Great," said the official. "Oh, you have a presentation? Did you bring handouts?"

"What are handouts?" I joked. Silence.

Pete saved me. "We have some handouts," he said, and began distributing hard copies around the table.

"I think regulators have a very difficult job," I began. "You are in charge of creating new laws—or interpreting existing laws—around these new blockchain investments. But it's hard to regulate the new."

I pulled up a map of the world on my laptop screen. "If you move too quickly, you might stifle innovation. Then all these great blockchain projects move overseas, which is already happening. Switzerland, Malta, Gibraltar—they're all trying to make their countries blockchain-friendly.

"On the other hand, if you act too late, then investors stand the risk of getting burned." Here I switched to a slide of the Great Depression. "The Securities Act of 1933 was created in response to the great stock market crash, when hundreds of thousands of ordinary investors lost billions of dollars.

"The only problem with the Securities Act of 1933," I continued, "is that it was written in 1933." I smiled. Nothing.

"Well, it was passed into law in 1933," said one of the government officials. "And written earlier."

"Thank you. The point is it needs an update. We need to reinvent the Securities Act."

"What do you propose?" asked the senior official.

"Now, we've been meeting with blockchain investors all year, and there is no question they *think* of these tokens like securities—like stocks. Everyone thinks they're going to buy low, sell high. But they bought high"—here I showed a graph of the recent altcoin market—"and they're selling low. This is because *they don't know what they're doing*."

I clicked to a picture of a herd of sheep. "Over the past year," I told them, "I have been on a mission to educate investors on this stuff. And I have seen firsthand how humans are sheep. All of us. We follow the crowd. Market's up, everyone wants to buy. Market's down, everyone wants to sell. Sheeple."

Click. Picture of overlapping zigzag patterns. "But to beat the market, you've got to bet *against* the market. You've got to zig when everyone is zagging. And that requires thinking for yourself."

I took a sip of my water, which was surprisingly cold and refreshing. These guys really nailed water.

"But how can investors think for themselves, when they don't have the training? And wasn't that the problem behind the Great Depression: investors pouring their life savings into a brand-new stock market they didn't understand?"

"There were a lot of factors behind the Great Depression," the junior official cut in. "Brokers were overleveraged. The economy was in decline—"

"Thank you," I interrupted. "The point is, how can we better educate investors?" I clicked to a slide that read "Investor Education." "Today we require *investor accreditation*, but I want to propose that we make laws around *investor education*. Here's how it might work."

Investor Education vs. Investor Accreditation

To prevent the ordinary investor from gambling his life savings on high-risk investments, the Securities Act of 1933 created a special class of **accredited investors**. To qualify today, you must have a net worth of at least $1 million (your house doesn't count), or make at least $200,000 per year.

In other words, the wealthy.

This old-fashioned idea, which has gradually been adopted around the globe, is that accredited investors know what they're doing. They can afford to make riskier investments: they're wealthy! But today, when information is plentiful and abundant, couldn't *everyone* know what they're doing?

Since blockchain investments are new, a central question is this: Will the government allow them to be sold to accredited investors only? Will it be blockchain for the wealthy, or blockchain for everyone?

Between 2017 and 2018, the flood of new blockchain tokens slowed to a trickle. Who wanted to create a blockchain token for the people, only to be told it was a high-risk investment available only to accredited investors? The price of bitcoin dropped. The market cooled. That trickle began to freeze.

To us, the way forward is obvious: change investor accreditation to **investor certification**. Take a series of investor courses, pass a test, and then you can be an accredited investor. This is how we issue driver's licenses—which are surely more dangerous, because lives are at stake!

Investor accreditation: In the United States and other countries, certain investments are only open to "accredited investors" (i.e., the wealthy).

We propose replacing this with **investor certification**—training and a test—that's open to everyone.

PLAIN ENGLISH
A B C

There is also a curious double standard: anyone can walk into a casino, day or night, and blow their kids' college fund—no license needed. You don't need to be accredited to play the lottery or buy scratch tickets: they're available at the gas station. Why isn't *gambling* available to accredited investors only?

If the government wants to protect its citizens from making stupid investments, the solution is simple: help them make smart ones.

"We require licenses for brokers, dealers, and financial advisers," I said, wrapping up my presentation. "Training and certification. Let's do the same for investors. Turn investor accreditation into investor certification. That levels the playing field. That makes it available to everyone."

I clicked to a stock photo of a protestor holding up a sign that read WE ARE THE 99%. "That opens up investing from the 1 percent to the 99 percent. And that opens up the pocketbooks of the 99 percent. That's good for the economy. That's good for everyone.

"Blockchain for everyone," I concluded, and sat down.

Big finish. Where there was usually applause, today there was only silence. In the corner, someone poured a glass of refreshing ice water.

"Were you rehearsing for a TED Talk?" Pete laughed a few hours later.

"I thought you were going to pass around a collection plate," Jade added, sipping her coffee. "Which we could use."

We were debriefing back at TechLab, sitting in the open workspace with blockchain developers and entrepreneurs buzzing all around us.

"They were smart," I observed. "They listened. But no one is in any hurry to take action. Meanwhile, we are in a world of hurry. Pete, what's the latest on the sales pipeline?"

"Lots of talk," Pete admitted, "but no action. We have a ton of leads, but half my day is spent weeding out the yahoos."

"What's up with our Polish energy drink?" I asked Jade.

"Contract is stuck with their CFO, Bartosz."

I sighed. "And we lost another legacy client this morning. Where are we with Sooyoung?"

"Still waiting on payment."

I fought down panic. "It's like we're flying a plane—the old business—while we're trying to build a new plane—the blockchain business." I placed my hands out, palms down, to show the two planes flying side by side, one of them quickly losing altitude.

"I'm worried we're trying to do too much," Jade stated flatly. "Two businesses, two websites, two teams . . . Too expensive."

"And what's the revenue model again?" Even Pete was losing his typical good humor. "That meeting today was great, but where's the money?"

"I don't know," I admitted. "But if we can influence policy—if we can help reinvent the financial markets—isn't that worth doing?"

"My job is to *sell*," Pete responded, regarding me through his glasses. "I get that we're flying one plane while we're building a new one. But the plane is going down."

For once, I didn't know what to say.

CHAPTER 24

The Gold Rush

"No poker tonight," announced Kirk, laying out a board game on green velvet. "We're playing Gold Digger."

"John should be good at this one." Ben half smiled at me.

"I need a refresher on the rules," Evan said, laying out the cards on the table.

"You place claims on these plots of land," Kirk explained, turning over a stack of cards one by one. "Some of the plots have fabulous wealth, and others"—he turned over another card—"have fool's gold."

"Did you know that, during the California Gold Rush, most people didn't get rich from mining gold?" Evan began. "They

Mining: Bitcoin (and some altcoins) are "mined," or produced, by computers solving math problems. In other words, the "miners" who contribute their power to the network are rewarded with tokens.

PLAIN ENGLISH
A B C

got rich selling picks and shovels to the miners at vastly inflated prices. You'd open a general store near a bunch of miners, sell them all this mining equipment at ten times cost."

"Isn't it kind of like bitcoin **mining**?" Ben asked. "The money's not in the mining; it's in providing services to the miners."

"Well, look who's been bitten by the bitcoin bug!" I exclaimed.

"So you contribute your computer to the bitcoin network, and you're rewarded with a little bit of bitcoin," Kirk clarified. "So why doesn't that make money? Seems like you're just paying for electricity."

"Competition," Ben replied, munching a nacho. "Just like the gold rush."

"Also, bitcoin has built-in scarcity," Evan explained. "Satoshi programmed it so that it becomes harder to mine bitcoin as time goes on. That makes it more expensive, so it uses a ton of electricity."

I looked at my friends in amazement. "Where did all this knowledge come from?"

Ben shrugged. "You know, the Internet."

"So is the value investor looking into blockchain now?" I asked him. "Have we converted you from Buffett to bitcoin?"

"Not converted, but considering." He took a swallow of beer. "But I think there may be an easier way of investing in blockchain."

"What's that?"

"Picks and shovels."

Picks and Shovels (and Everything Else)

In 1849, California went insane.[42]

It all started the year before when a carpenter named James W. Marshall was hired to build a sawmill on the bank of the American River, near present-day Sacramento. One day he was checking out the channel below the mill when some bright, shiny flakes caught his eye.

He picked up a few pieces and looked at them carefully. He knew enough about minerals to suspect what he had just discovered. He pressed the flakes together and found they could be molded into different shapes. He gathered up a handful, then approached a fellow carpenter who was working on building the mill wheel.

"I have found it," said Marshall.

"What is it?" asked his coworker.

"Gold!"[43]

Thus started the California Gold Rush, a collective hysteria that is hard to comprehend today. More than three hundred thousand people flooded into California from all over the world. Driven mad by "gold fever," people abandoned their families, cashed in their life savings, and risked everything.

Getting there by land was bad enough: the two-thousand-mile journey by covered wagon was fraught with diseases, robbers, and the perpetual stink of animals left to die on the trail. ("You have died of dysentery.")

Getting there by sea was no picnic, either: a six-month journey from the East Coast, with occasional stops in disease-infested foreign lands, and near-constant hunger and thirst. Once they reached California, so many crews simply jumped ship that the ports were choked with abandoned boats.

If you made it to California alive, you found a swollen mass of humanity facing deplorable living conditions and stratospheric prices. If you wanted to buy a tent or basic mining equipment, it might cost ten times what you would have paid for it back home. Many slept on blankets under trees.

Worse, all the easy gold had already been mined. If there was a riverbed that looked promising, it was already teeming with people, every speck of gold picked clean. You found that miners were now using specialized equipment like cradles and sluices. Some were even experimenting with hydraulic mining.

Some people did get rich selling "picks and shovels," but that's only part of the story. It's better to say that the gold rush created a ridiculous amount of business opportunity far beyond the gold itself.

Many successful entrepreneurs simply created service businesses. The miners needed haircuts and doctors and tax accountants. They needed groceries and saloons and brothels. They needed laborers: metalworkers and carpenters and blacksmiths.

The gold rush kicked off a frenzy in railroad stocks. Investors saw that miners would need a way to easily transport all that new wealth to New York, which eventually drove a second wave of gold fever, this time in railroad companies.

To say that "picks and shovels" were the only two moneymaking opportunities is to miss the broader point: there were a thousand possible investments, a whole ecosystem of opportunity.

The gold rush is incredibly similar to the blockchain boom. Like the gold of the Forty-Niners, bitcoin is also "mined," though it's by high-end computers performing extremely complex computations. In the early days, you could mine bitcoin on your home computer—but now it is done in enormous server farms.

The characters you meet in the blockchain world remind me of what the early miners must have been like: hard-charging entrepreneurs who are as colorful as a carnival show. Also, the valuations of companies that specialize in blockchain are about ten times what you'd expect to pay.

This means *there are many blockchain investments that don't require buying bitcoin or altcoins.* These are traditional, publicly traded companies that will benefit from the blockchain bonanza: the "picks and shovels" of our modern-day gold rush. Here are a few investing ideas.

The mining equipment: specialized hardware companies. Early gold miners used simple pans to sift through rocks and silt in riverbeds, hoping to find telltale flecks of gold. Then came inventions like the gold cradle, which took in huge quantities of river mud, "rocking" away the debris to find gold.

Similarly, bitcoin could once be "mined" using your desktop PC, but today's specialized computers—or "mining rigs"—are built for mathematical speed, packed with high-end graphics cards (like the ones used by serious videogamers), which specialize in extremely fast calculations.

Consider investing in companies like **Nvidia** and **AMD**, which specialize in these graphics cards and chips. Also consider companies that make application-specific integrated circuits (ASICs), which are processors built exclusively for mining bitcoin. **Taiwan Semiconductor** and **Samsung** are two major players in ASICs built for blockchain. (Bonus: ASICs are also being used in AI.)

The infrastructure: tech companies betting on blockchain. Like most financial revolutions, the California Gold Rush was led by scrappy entrepreneurs and aggressive speculators—not by large, conservative companies. Still, the old-school companies that saw change on the horizon were able to profit from it.

Some of today's biggest tech companies see blockchain on the horizon. For example, **IBM** has taken a leadership role in the development of Hyperledger, an open-source blockchain project that has attracted other well-known technology companies like **Cisco**, **Fujitsu**, **Hitachi**, **NEC**, and **VMware**.

Look for companies that are building out real blockchain divisions and contributing meaningfully to the ecosystem, not just paying lip service to blockchain technology. Although blockchain may well destroy their core businesses, this early R&D may help them reinvent themselves.

The experts: blockchain consulting companies. Huge veins of gold were trapped in cliff faces and pillars of rock. Specialized engineers developed methods of hydraulic mining, or blasting high-pressure water to chip away at the rock. You better believe those dudes weren't cheap.

Today, finding good blockchain developers is like finding good wizards: programming on the blockchain is a dark art known by a very few. Most schools aren't teaching it yet. Skilled developers with blockchain experience can name their own price and pick their own projects.

Similarly, good blockchain consultants are few and far between. This is a magnificent opportunity, as everyone from insurance companies to petroleum refineries is trying to figure out their blockchain strategy—and they don't understand the first thing about the technology.

Traditional consulting companies like **Accenture** and development companies like **Infosys** stand to benefit from the demand in specialized blockchain knowledge. There will be many other specialist shops to give them a run for their money.

The intellectual property: companies with blockchain patents. What if that carpenter James Marshall had kept his discovery to himself? What if he had just quietly mined gold on his lunch break, never telling a soul? Better yet, what if he had bought the land, then issued mining licenses for the land where he found the gold?

Public companies are rushing to file their own blockchain patents, according to a report from intellectual property research firm Envision IP.[44] These blockchain patents may be worth billions of dollars of future revenue, if other companies end up licensing them.

Consider investing in companies holding these patents, because they're serious about the technology: the leaders are **Bank of America**, **IBM**, **Mastercard**, **TD Bank**, and **Accenture**. (Note that big technology companies like Google, Apple, and Microsoft don't currently make the top ten.)

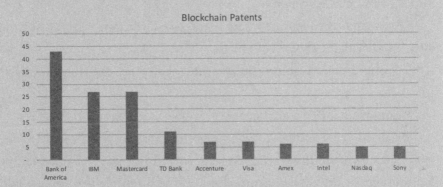

Blockchain Patents

The money movers: financial services companies. Some of the most successful gold rush entrepreneurs created banks in order to provide financing, store wealth, and exchange cash for gold. In fact, the venerable Wells Fargo started during the gold rush, and it's dabbling in blockchain today.[45]

The chart above shows just how seriously other big financial institutions are taking blockchain. You can also consider smaller players like the payment processor **Square**, which has a government-approved license to accept bitcoin payments.

You might even consider nontraditional companies like discount retailer **Overstock.com**, which was among the first to accept bit-coin and is increasingly shifting its focus to blockchain. The financial juggernauts of tomorrow are likely to look very different from those today. (Who could have predicted PayPal?)

"So that's what I've been doing with my Fridays," Ben summed up. "One day a week I research the companies that will provide the 'picks and shovels' to blockchain."

"Are we going to play or what?" Kirk asked. He tapped at his hearing aid. "I only caught about half of that."

"Deal out dem dadburn cards!" I hollered in my old-timey prospector's voice.

"Consarn it," Ben added gently.

I paused for a moment, regarding the cards in front of me. They were facedown, unknown, existing in a quantum state of uncertainty. Schrödinger's cards. When I turned them over, multiple timelines would collapse into a singular reality where I would see what I was holding.

"What you got, hoss?" Kirk prodded.

Ben's approach made so much sense. Why tie up your net worth in blockchain technology, which was still buggy and hard to use? Why not just invest in the companies that were investing in blockchain?

I looked at my cards, which were still facedown. Was I holding a pile of riches, or fool's gold?

CHAPTER 25

Breaking the Chain

It was a very big, very British day. The Lord Mayor of London was coming to TechLab!

One of the world's oldest offices, the Right Honourable the Lord Mayor of London is an elected position that serves to represent and promote businesses and individuals in London. The Lord Mayor, along with a delegation of banking and financial leaders, was stopping by our incubator to learn about blockchain.

We had prepared exhaustively for the event, lining up a panel of Boston's best and brightest. I had been up all night prepping my presentation. I was making last-minute arrangements with the team in TechLab's common area, where the caterers were setting out food, when Benedict approached me.

"Could I have a word?" he asked.

"Let's make sure this room is a hive of activity today," I instructed the team as I stood up. "And have the photographer get pictures over to Cliff for sharing on social media ASAP." I turned to Benedict, who weirdly was not smiling. "Big day!" I exclaimed, clapping him on the shoulder.

"Let's talk." He led me to a small meeting room and we pulled up chairs. Still no smile. This was bad.

"You look tired," he began.

"Well, thank you." I smiled. "Every day brings us a little closer to death."

"Listen—"

"I am actually glad we're having this chat," I interrupted him, "because I have an idea."

He hesitated. "Okay."

"This blockchain incubator is the talk of the town," I told him. "Last week I was contacted by TechLab offices in Silicon Valley and London. They both want to build blockchain hubs in their locations."

"Yes, I heard that."

"But last night I had an even bigger idea, an idea that will double the market value of TechLab." I pulled out my Moleskine notebook. "You know how we have TechLab credits, right?"

"Yes."

"Every month you pay your membership fee, you get TechLab credits that you can use to book conference rooms or buy food at any TechLab worldwide. *That is a currency.* We already have our own currency! The idea is to put TechLab credits on the blockchain, to make it a digital currency."

I opened my Moleskine notebook. "This came to me at 4:00 a.m., but I'll put it into slides so we can present it to your CEO."

A Rewarding Idea

I f blockchain is a technology that lets us share value, how about letting us share all those valuable rewards points? Frequent-flier miles, coffee cards, shopping points—these are all "virtual currencies," little economic systems that businesses create to encourage your loyalty.

You probably have a wallet full of these cards. Coffee points: Buy nine coffees, get the tenth one free. Supermarket points. Gas points. Retailer points. Credit card points.

What if we set all these points free?

Imagine you're trying to book a holiday with frequent-flier points. You have 40,000 points but you need 50,000 to buy the ticket. The airline will sell you 10,000 at a ridiculous price, but what if you could buy the points on a public market?

Better yet, what if these rewards points were interchangeable? What if you could give up 10,000 of your supermarket points and receive 10,000 frequent-flier points in return?

Behind the scenes, a blockchain (we'll call it RewardChain) will "buy" the 10,000 supermarket points from you, then transfer them into a common token (we'll call it RewardCoin). Then you use your RewardCoin to purchase the 10,000 points you need for your flight.

Think of this like converting dollars to pounds at a currency exchange kiosk. The currency exchange company is actually "buying" dollars and "selling" pounds, but this is invisible: all you see is dollars being converted to pounds, minus a service fee.

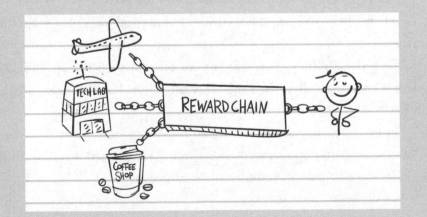

RewardChain will require buy-in from companies, as most don't allow customers to transfer points between each other. But the rewards of RewardChain will outweigh the risks: every retailer who participates in a decentralized marketplace like RewardChain gets exposed to more shoppers. It's like a mall.

To be sure, retailers will have to carefully manage the redemption rates for their loyalty points so they don't lose money giving away free coffee and free flights. It won't be easy, but those who figure it out first will be amply rewarded.

Benedict interrupted me. "Look, you're a charismatic speaker. But today is your last day at TechLab."

Full body blow. I stared at him, stunned.

"It's not working out," he continued. "It's not a good fit."

"It's not a good fit." I mouthed the words.

"So we'd like your company to start cleaning out your office immediately. We'll have our security detail help you move out your things."

"Security," I repeated. "Because we are so dangerous."

"They'll help you use the security elevator and we can handle this quietly."

"Security? Really?" This was the kicker. I had just been knocked unconscious in an alley, then my assailant felt he should pour garbage on me.

"In exchange for an early termination of our agreement, I've been authorized to offer you this compensation." He pushed a release form my way and pointed to a number at the bottom.

I swallowed.

"We can tell everyone we decided to go our separate ways," Benedict continued, placing a pen in front of me.

"Back up." I shook my head. "What is happening?"

"Look," he sighed. "The endless parade of visitors. The street sign. The video studio. You are constantly doing things without permission. You act like you own this place."

"Well, I did help you find half your tenants."

"And we appreciate that. But you don't own the place."

"I know. *I pay you*, remember?"

"We will prorate the rest of your monthly membership—"

"Hang on." I skimmed over the legalese, trying to think coherently. "There's a confidentiality clause. So you want to pay me off in exchange for my silence?"

He grimaced. "I wouldn't put it that way."

"Do you think," I asked, "looking back, that you will consider this the single biggest mistake of your career?"

"Just sign the agreement"—he pushed the pen toward me—"and we can go our separate ways."

I looked at the number they were offering. It was tempting. "And if I don't?"

He hesitated. "You're still leaving."

"*Do you have any idea what is happening out there?*" I boiled. "The Lord Mayor of London is due to arrive in a few minutes. They are looking at best practices for starting their own blockchain incubator. So if *you* would like to make the blockchain presentation, then be my guest."

He gritted his laser-chiseled teeth, forming perfect rows. "I want you out by the end of the day."

"One more thing." I tore the legal contract in half. "I can't be bought."

I went to a private office and locked myself inside. What would I tell everyone? Where would we go? How would we rebuild? This blockchain incubator, lovingly built to nurture these little eggs, had been flash-frozen. Because *Benedict had unplugged the power cord.*

I brushed away tears and steeled myself for the two-hour seminar on blockchain, one of the most important moments of my professional career. My voice choked as I ironically rehearsed my opening line. "*This is the greatest time to be alive.*"

CHAPTER 26

The Bubble Bursts

Over the next few months, we got to be real connoisseurs of office lobbies.

Every financial building in Boston now has a coffee shop in its downstairs lobby. The Starbucks at One Financial Center was bustling but cramped; the Blue Bottle Coffee at 100 Federal Street was airy but chilly. Today our remaining team sat huddled around our laptops for warmth while cold rain washed down in sheets outside.

I looked at our little crew of digital nomads, all that was left of my company. No one would take us, as coworking spaces were fearful of the word "cryptocurrency." Mailchimp, our email provider, had canceled our account because we used the word "bitcoin." They needn't have worried: the price of bitcoin was in free fall, and investors were fleeing.

"A ray of hope," I offered to Pete. "Sales lead. Looks like the real deal."

I turned my laptop so we could both see the email, adjusting the font size to 300 percent for Pete's sake. "We would like Media Shower to help us promote our new blockchain token PowerUpCoin," I read, "which will increase in value as more people join."

"So a pyramid scheme," Pete responded.

"It's not a pyramid scheme," I argued, reading from the website. "PowerUpCoin is designed to increase in value over time by **burning** tokens as they are traded. The faster transactions happen, the more tokens are burned and the faster the price rises."

"The more *investors* are burned," Pete muttered.

"So they're trying to create more scarcity, so that more people use the token, until . . . what?" I pondered this. "Only one person is left?"

"Like a pyramid scheme," Pete repeated.

"The website looks legit," I responded, clicking through pages. "But what does the token actually *do*?"

"This is what's so hard." Pete pointed. "It's all so new. You look at this site, even *you* think it's real. Look at this: 'We have built-in anti-fraud prevention measures to ensure the integrity of every token.' What does that even *mean*?"

> **Burning:** destroying a blockchain token permanently. For example, burning might be done to decrease supply, in an attempt to stimulate a higher price. Think of burning as the opposite of creating tokens or "printing money." (See **The Parable of the Goldbuckians**, page 268.)

"It looks like the token does nothing," I deflated.

"The logo even looks like a pyramid!" Pete pointed out, laughing.

"No, it's like an upward arrow." I squinted. "You know, PowerUp-Coin."

"*It's a pyramid!*"

"Do we have anything real in the pipeline?" I asked, rubbing my eyes and shivering.

"It is a sea of chaos," Pete replied. "All noise, no signal." He turned his laptop around to face me. "Here's our sales pipeline. Two hundred leads in the past month. *Maybe* two of these are real."

"What do people want?" I asked.

"They all want to buy articles on *Bitcoin Market Journal*."

"Not going to do that," I stated flatly.

"I know. But it's how this industry works, John. All the other block-chain sites are pay to play. Send them a bitcoin, they'll write a nice article about PowerUpCoin."

"We've got to build trust," I maintained. "In blockchain, those that build trust will thrive. Those that don't will die."

"Maybe it's time to reconsider advertising," Pete suggested for the umpteenth time.

"Advertising is a crack pipe. We take one hit, we'll never get off." And once again I launched into my spiel.

Stop the Adness

In his final column, *New York Times* tech columnist Farhad Manjoo stated, "The Internet ad business lies at the heart of just about every terrible thing online."[46]

Ads interrupt your experience, slow down your computer, and crash your browser. Ads install spyware in the form of tracking code called "cookies" (itself a deceptive term, because cookies are delicious). Then companies track your every move, which is how ads follow you around the Internet.

In the world of blockchain investing, many websites will write better articles, or give you more coverage, if you buy their ads. We don't trust the media, in part because we don't know what's editorial and what's advertorial.

All these problems come down to ads.

It wasn't supposed to be this way. The original architects of the World Wide Web thought that micropayments—payments of less than a dollar—would be how the web was monetized.

You're probably familiar with the "404 error," when a page is not found on the Internet. The "402 error" was the error you'd get when a payment was required. *The 402 predated the 404.* Have you ever seen a 402 error? No, because we didn't get micropayments. We got ads.

Plenty of micropayment systems have been tried and failed because of what bitcoin pioneer Nick Szabo calls "mental trans-action costs."[47] If it costs twenty-five cents to continue reading a *New York Times* article, you have to mentally compare it to other articles, other websites, what you could buy with . . . *Forget it: I'll just check BuzzFeed instead.*

The more we have to think about paying for something, the less likely we are to pay for it. That's why Amazon invented 1-Click ordering. Doesn't get any lower-friction than that—not until Jeff Bezos invents the 1-Thought, which is an Internet-connected hat that will buy something as soon as you desire it.

Today, subscriptions work better than micropayments, because they eliminate that mental friction. One price: all you can eat. *New York Times*: all you can read. HBO: all you can watch.

But blockchain can make micropayments work by making them invisible. I will explain this simply, using fairy tales.

———

Take the Massachusetts Turnpike. This is the main highway leading into and out of Boston, and it's a toll road. Back in the day, you had tollbooths, which snarled up traffic and made everyone resentful.

You're already commuting in rush hour traffic, and now you've got to pay to *use the road.*

The tollbooth collectors had the worst job in the world, dealing with grumpy commuters every day, so they got grumpy as well. In fairy tales, you know the troll who guards the bridge and says, *"Three gold coins!"*? Why is he always grumpy? Because he has to deal with all the commuters!

Then, a few years ago, they tore down the tollbooths. Gone. Now you have this little device in your car—a transponder—that automatically charges your account. I'm not talking about an automated tollbooth. There is no booth.

It's as if they removed the troll and replaced him with a robot with a radar. You don't even know that it's happening. You've got this online account that you load up with fifty bucks, and it just draws down against that account. Zero friction. It's invisible. It's incredible.

That is brilliant engineering, and that is what blockchain-based micropayments can look like.

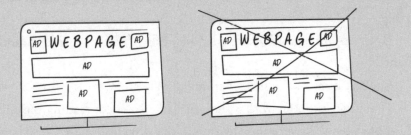

Blockchain can help us stop the adness.

Let's imagine a project called ContentChain that lets you buy a token called ContentCoin. You load up your ContentCoin account with $50, and as you browse the Web, it seamlessly pulls ContentCoin from the sites you visit most, paying it back to the publisher.[48]

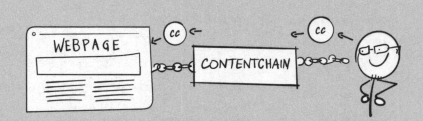

To make these ideas work, we need an open-source block-chain that's easy for publishers to use and easy for users to install as a browser extension. Most importantly, we've got to have great content. This is how Netflix, Amazon, and HBO have built great networks without advertising: by producing content so good that people are willing to buy it.

"Right," Pete said, "but we need revenue *now*. So how about advertising?"

"I hate to interrupt," Jade added helpfully, "but we just lost another client."

Another blow of the sledgehammer. "Why?"

"They're taking the work in-house." Jade frowned, reading the email. "Also, they see that we're moving in another direction with blockchain."

As I watched the rain beat down outside, I pictured our company plane losing altitude. Lightning crackled around its nose cone as it began to brush the tops of trees, searching for a place to land. I pictured myself running between the cockpit and the passengers, trying to keep the plane in the air while also serving drinks.

My shoes were still soaked, and I started to shiver.

Pete noticed. "Let's get you a warm-up," he said.

"I've had enough coffee."

"I'll buy," he replied, smiling. "We've got to keep buying stuff as long as we're working here."

We stepped away from the team, and Pete spoke in a low voice. "Listen. I don't know how to say this, so I'll come out and say it."

My stomach dropped, but I kept a poker face. "What's up?"

"I got offered another job."

"Oof." I grabbed a nearby chair for support.

"I know things are going more slowly than expected with the new business . . ."

"I don't know how to say this," I responded, "so I'll come out and say it. I haven't been paid all year."

"Oof." Pete and I both sat down, out of earshot of the others.

"I really thought we were going to go to the moon," Pete said, smiling.

The moon, I thought, wondering how this would all end. *Right now, we're just trying to keep this thing from exploding on the launchpad.*

CHAPTER 27

Private Parts

My life was steeped in irony. Here I was, speaking at a blockchain conference in London, completely unable to build a business out of blockchain. The blockchain industry itself, built on the idea of decentralization, seemed unable to move forward without permission from a centralized government.

And my most trusted adviser was a Canadian.

"What's it been, aboot a year?" asked Richard Kastelein, dressed as always in his signature black T-shirt, black hair swept up in a swoop.

"Feels like a decade." I shook his hand.

"That's blockchain time," he noted as I sat down. "One year in this industry is like seven years everywhere else. It's like dog years, eh?"

"Eh," I replied.

"So you've been busy. I see you all over LinkedIn."

"On one hand, things have never been better. It's crazy. I got a book deal."

"Congratulations!"

"On the other hand, it's a nightmare. We are just not able to get traction on the blockchain business."

"What are you trying to do?"

"Everything."

"Well, maybe that's the problem. Maybe you're doing too much."

"I'm definitely doing too much." As we sat in the lunch area on the convention floor, I opened my salad and started to eat. "How about you?"

"Just started Decentralized Pictures. It's like Kickstarter for movies. You can fund a new film by investing in our token, which can increase in value as the film becomes successful. This lets everyone invest in creative ideas they care about."

"That's a great idea," I said, suddenly ravenous. "Maybe we'll turn my book into a movie."

"Yeah, and Francis Ford Coppola is involved. Pretty exciting."

I angrily stuffed salad into my mouth. *How did he get Francis Ford Coppola?*

"All this stuff is pretty simple," he said. "It's really just about building community."

I chewed on this while I chewed on lettuce.

"The blockchain is about people," he told me again. "Get them onto your blockchain, the value of your token goes up. If you don't—no traction, no trading—the value goes down. I just help people build those communities."

"We're trying to build this community of blockchain investors," I said between mouthfuls. "But when the price of bitcoin dropped, they all fled for the exit."

"Sounds aboot right," Richard laughed. "That's like any market, isn't it? But there's always opportunity."

"Oh, no." I looked into my salad with horror.

"What?"

"Are those pine nuts?"

"What's a pine nut?"

"I am deathly allergic to pine nuts."

"You mean peanuts?"

"No, pine nuts. From the pine tree. Oh, boy. Who puts pine nuts on a trade show salad?"

"Well, you are in Europe."

"Oh, no." I put my head on the table. "I've got to go onstage in half an hour."

"Do you need me to call an ambulance or something?"

I pulled out my phone and googled "anaphylaxis reaction time." *Between three and thirty minutes.*

"Do you want to go to the washroom? Stick your finger down your throat?"

"Maybe I didn't eat a pine nut," I said hopefully, fishing around the salad.

"What happens when you eat them?" he asked.

"Bad things." I remembered the one emergency room visit, decades ago. I barely made it to the hospital in time, my face swelling up and my lungs closing down. It was an eight-hour horror show.

"Do you carry an EpiPen?"

"In my hotel room." My thoughts careened wildly. "It's twenty years old."

"I think we should get you to a hospital."

I sat still for a moment, scanning my body for any sign of reaction. No itchiness. No swelling. No shortage of breath. *Maybe I got lucky.*

"I'm going to deliver this talk," I decided.

"What, in half an hour? That's crazy," Richard laughed. "Imagine if you go into shock at the podium."

"I came all the way to London and I'm going on that stage," I vowed.

Richard looked at me with raised eyebrows as if to say, *It's your funeral.*

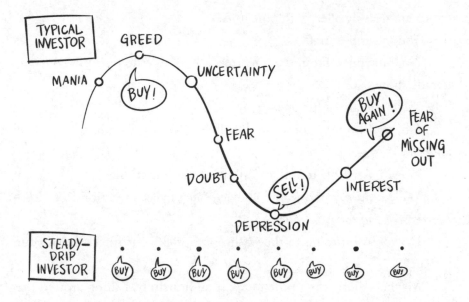

"'Should I buy bitcoin?'" I addressed the crowd half an hour later. "This is the question we hear most frequently from beginning blockchain investors. I'm not a financial adviser, so I can't give you advice, but *yes.*"

The crowd chuckled. If I seemed a little less animated than usual, it was because I was monitoring my lips and tongue for a life-threatening allergic reaction. The mouth and face would be the first to go, followed by the lungs and heart. I had located the nearest hospital and put the number on speed dial.

"The easy answer is yes," I added. "Use a service like Coinbase.com and buy a little bit of bitcoin—even if it's only £100—so you have some skin in the game. The process of buying it will be instructive. You'll start following its price. Soon you'll be reading everything you can about blockchain, and your friends will be begging you to shut up." Another laugh.

I clicked to a slide showing Benjamin Graham's classic book *The Intelligent Investor*. "Here's Benjamin Graham, the guy who taught Warren Buffett how to invest. He invented the concept of 'value investing,' which we're bringing into the age of bitcoin."

A hand shot up. "Warren Buffett called bitcoin 'rat poison,'" said a hefty bearded gentleman.

"Rat poison squared," someone else helpfully chimed in.

My mouth was itching. *Or was it?* Trick or sick?

"Rat poison squared," I repeated. "That is rat poison times rat poison. But if we *divide* rat poison by rat poison, we get one." This made no sense. "I have the greatest respect for Mr. Buffett, but I respectfully disagree. May I continue?"

Silence. I could feel my heart throbbing. Nerves or nervous shutdown?

"With any blockchain investing strategy, the first step is to invest the same amount each month," I continued. "Decide how much you can afford to invest— whether that's £50 or £5,000—and put aside that money each month, preferably through automatic withdrawal.

"This process is called dollar-cost averaging in the U.S., pound-cost averaging in the UK, but I call it **steady-drip investing**. When the market is up, your monthly investment buys less. When the market is down, it buys more. But you're averaging over time through that slow and steady *drip, drip, drip*."

Steady-drip investing: investing the same amount each month, regardless of market conditions.

Also known as "dollar-cost averaging," it protects you from investing on emotion.

KEY TERM

Heavyset raised his hand again. "Dollar cost averaging doesn't work," he scoffed. "Just google it. No one advises that anymore."

I was starting to sweat: a bad sign. *Flop sweat or drop dead?* "There's a lot of research comparing a single lump-sum investment to steady-drip investing," I agreed, "so if you have 100,000 pounds to invest today, by all means. Do you have 100,000 pounds?"

There were some chuckles. I didn't intend the double meaning.

"For most of us, we have to invest money as we earn it," I continued. "What is an IRA savings account but a steady-drip investment in your retirement portfolio? Auto-withdrawals from your paycheck? Steady-drip investing."

Now I was sweating for sure: steady drip in-my-vesting. "Academically, lump-sum investing is best—but we don't live in academia; we live in the real world. And most of us need help with the discipline of investing. A little each month, *drip drip drip.* Slow and steady wins the race.

"More importantly," I soldiered on, "investing the same amount each month protects you from yourself: you're not caught up in the manic-depressive mood swings of other investors, the roller coaster of crypto-craziness. Steady-drip investing is a powerful psychological advantage.

"When people ask you how the blockchain market is doing, you can say what the financial columnist Jason Zweig calls the seven most powerful words for value investors: 'I don't know and I don't care.' "[49]

I mopped my forehead with a tissue. "My vision," I said as my vision blurred, "is that we will have a user-friendly blockchain investing service. Auto-withdrawals from your bank account each month. Auto-allocation to the top altcoins. So easy that your grandmother can do it. Blockchain for everyone."

Time to go. I didn't stick around for questions, just grabbed my bag and headed for the convention center door, dialing an Uber as I jogged.

———

When you enter an emergency room with your face swollen like a tomato, they don't make you wait. They did present me with a form, which I signed without thinking. They rushed me into a bed, and I instantly had a doctor checking my vitals.

"What did you eat?" he asked.

"Pide duts."

"Peanuts?"

"Pide duts," I spat. My tongue was thick and swollen. "From da pide tree."

"You ate nuts from a tree?"

"I thig I'm going to black out," I told him. I had that light-headed feeling like when you stand up too fast, only I was in bed.

"Your blood pressure is dangerously low," he said, violently grabbing my belt and ripping my pants down around my ankles.

At just that moment the curtain around me pulled back to reveal two sexy British nurses. I'm sure they weren't trying to be sexy, but in my impending coma, that's how it seemed. I was wearing, like, the most embarrassing underwear imaginable. Tighty whiteys, but not so tight and not so white.

The doctor injected adrenaline into my thigh, and I almost instantly felt better. It was incredible. "Dat is a wonder drug," I marveled.

"Your body is using all its resources to fight off the allergen," he said. "We'll get you some diphenhydramine." The sexy nurses ran off, closing the curtain behind them.

"Bedadryl?" I asked him. "Just an EpiPen ad Bedadryl?"

"You're lucky you made it here," he said. "Did you take an Uber?"

"You doe," I continued, only half-aware of what I was saying, "you don't deed to store sedsitive medical data in a cedtradized datadase. Do you doe about blockchain?"

"Take these," he said, handing me a couple of pills. "And stop talking."

Privacy Is a Human Right

It's common sense that we want privacy in a medical office, where our private parts are quite literally exposed—so why don't we demand the same privacy with our medical records, where everything else is exposed?

> Identity is a pain point. I don't believe in universal identifiers, because they can allow surveillance and things like that. But with blockchain, you don't need government-issued identification: people can be their own password.[50]
> —Dr. John Henry Clippinger, MIT Media Lab

THOUGHT LEADER

Our medical records are the most private of our private information, and they should be our personal property. That goes for all our other private information: our height, weight, marital status, ethnicity, financial history, and so on. No one should be allowed to access these things without our permission.

Consider that when a young woman goes to a bar, she is asked to show her driver's license, with all her personal information, to a meathead bouncer. The bouncer only needs to verify her birth date, but the woman's license exposes everything—including her home address.

Now imagine the bouncer enters her home address into a

spreadsheet. After doing this for a few weeks, he sells the spreadsheet to other bouncers to help them bounce better. Now every bouncer knows where she lives.

For years, the credit reporting company Equifax has gathered far more information than our hypothetical bouncer. The company has collected personal financial data on millions of Americans— birth dates, Social Security numbers, salaries—all without permission.

Then Equifax lost it all in 2017 when hackers breached its centralized database, stealing the private data of at least 143 million Americans.[51] The crime is not just that hackers stole the data. The crime is also that Equifax was allowed to gather the data in the first place.

"Identity theft" is a buzzword everyone knows, because it's happening so often. Blockchain provides a solution, in the form of **identity tokens**. Let's imagine a new blockchain app called IdentityChain, where you securely upload all your personal information: everything from your medical records to your employment history.

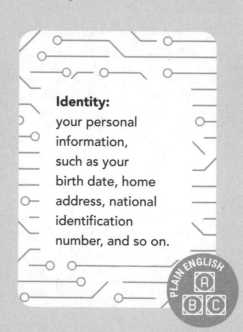

Identity: your personal information, such as your birth date, home address, national identification number, and so on.

PLAIN ENGLISH Ⓐ Ⓑ Ⓒ

When providers want that information, you can share it with them—either for free (like your doctor) or for a fee (like a credit reporting agency), with them paying you in IdentityCoins.

Privacy is a human right, because no one wants their private parts exposed.

"Why don't you get some rest," said the British doctor, who seemed bathed in light. Woozy, I looked under the blanket, where my pants were still gathered around my ankles.

"Dighty whiteys," I giggled.

"What's that?"

"Nighty nighty." I was quickly asleep.

CHAPTER 28

Glass and the Abyss

Elon Musk once said that being an entrepreneur—at its worst moments—is like chewing glass and staring into the abyss.[52] Today that seemed like an understatement.

Jade and I were at the bank, requesting one more extension on our line of credit. All our credit had been exhausted, and we were down to our last month of cash. Everything—the bank accounts, the business, the house—was on the line.

How the heck did we get here?

"Hey." I placed my hand on hers. "We have each other."

She smiled. "We have each other."

"Grateful for you."

She rested her head on my shoulder. "You too."

"Well, top o' the morning." The Irish accent warmed me up. "I don't normally say that, but I know you like it."

"Sean. It's good to see a friendly face." Jade smiled and shook his hand.

"A pleasure to see you." He stopped when he saw me. "You look tired."

"Thanks so much."

He inspected my face more closely. "You okay? What happened?"

"I got hit in the face with a branch," I replied.

"Well, step into my office," he said, "and let's see what we can do."

The mood inside was heavy. "Sean, we've managed our cash the best we can," Jade began, "but we've had several clients default on us . . ."

"Including *your bank*," I put in, wincing at the thought of Sooyoung.

"I've got twelve-month cash projections," Jade continued, handing him a budget report, "with a plan to get us back into the black. But we need another extension."

Sean looked over the budget, frowning. "Bit of a tough year, then?"

You have no idea, I thought, my eyes welling up.

Sean glanced at me, then quickly looked away. "How did this happen?"

"We saw our business slowing down, so we tried to reinvent ourselves," Jade summarized.

"How?"

"We moved into blockchain," I replied.

"What's blockchain?"

Jade and I were both silent for a moment. "Do you want to take this one?" she asked me.

"Sean, do you remember back when we bought bitcoin?"

"Oh, yeah. How did that work out?"

"Still one of the best investments I've ever made."

"So why don't you just sell some of that? You can sell it, right?"

Jade looked at me, eyebrows raised.

"I believe in it long term."

"But you've got some short-term issues here." He pointed to the spreadsheet. "You've got liquidity; why not use it?"

"But it's *your bank* that has not paid us," I argued. "Do you know how much they owe us?" I pointed to the number on the spreadsheet.

Sean whistled. "So why don't you go to court for it?"

"We tried!"

"The legal fees are listed here." Jade pointed at a line item. "We're paying those down as well."

"What we need," I told him, "is a blockchain-based arbitration system."

"Not the time or place," Jade urged.

I pulled out my Moleskine notebook anyway.

Blockchain Arbitration: The $100,000 Idea

Let's say, purely for the sake of argument, that a client owes you $100,000.

The challenge of paying for services is that no one wants to pay up front. You hire a guy to do your roof, there's no way you're going to pay for the entire roof in advance.

The usual solution is to pay at milestones: Let's say 50 percent when the roof is half done, and 50 percent when the project is complete. But even this is not ideal, because the roofer can still get screwed on the last half. What's he going to do if you don't pay, tear the roof off that sucker?

The solution is a blockchain-based escrow system, like our balloon animal example but with a twist. You and the roofer enter into a smart contract, and you put in the entire cost of the roof up front. Right away this is a better system, because he knows you're good for it. Psychologically you're all in.

Now let's say there is disagreement. The roofer says the project is done, but you say the roof is leaking. The two of you go back and forth, but can't come to an agreement. The $100,000 (it's a big roof) sits in the smart contract, like escrow. You won't release it, but you won't get it back, either.

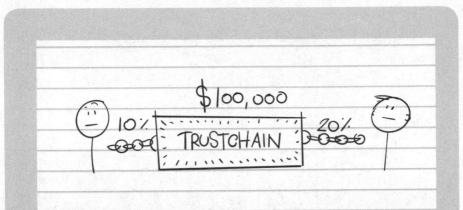

Let's say that this is all happening on a payment blockchain called TrustChain. When there's disagreement on a payment, each party **stakes** a percentage they're willing to pay for arbitration—in other words, how much you're each willing to "give up" to resolve the dispute.

Now that staking percentage goes to a decentralized arbitration committee (i.e., people who make a living from resolving TrustChain disputes). They work with the two of you to find a solution, and the members of the committee get paid the amount you've staked.

Staking: to "lock up" a set amount of money or tokens in exchange for some benefit.

Think of it like the "hold" a hotel will put on your credit card: you get the money back as long as you don't trash the room.

For example, you stake 10 percent of the $100,000, and the

roofer stakes 20 percent (he has more to lose, as he's already paid for the materials and labor). The arbitrators hear both sides of the story, view photos of the work, and review the roofer's previous TrustChain feedback (42 positive ratings) and your feedback (you're new). They rule in favor of the roofer, who's paid $70,000, and the arbitrators split the $30,000 stake.

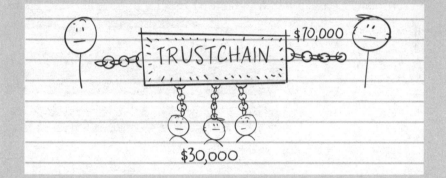

Keep in mind there is no centralized "company" managing all this! It is not like asking Visa to reverse a credit card charge or taking somebody to court: this is a decentralized system managed by the people. No lawyers needed.

"That's interesting," Sean murmured distractedly, "but I don't think there's anything more we can do." He put down the budgets. "You're pretty much tapped out."

In my head I pictured hurling a sledgehammer into the walls of Sean's office, letting forth a primal scream as shards of glass flew around me in slow motion.

"Unless . . ." Sean spun around to his computer and tapped a few keys. Jade and I sat forward, holding our breath.

"No." He looked back at us. "You're pretty much tapped out."

I chewed another mouthful of glass. "Maybe we sell the bitcoin," I sighed to Jade.

"You're already paying a load of interest," Sean reasoned. "It doesn't make sense to take on more debt. You've got liquidity. Just use it!"

I looked over at Jade. Her face had gone white.

"You okay?" I asked her. She handed me her phone, her eyes brimming with tears.

> I am so sorry to break the news this way, but I cannot make phone calls from the hospital.

> Your brother Joel passed away this morning.

CHAPTER 29

Goodbye

"Life," I began, "is difficult."

I looked around the small funeral home, filled with family and friends. Jade was there in the front row with her family, all the kids and grandkids. Kirk, Ben, and Evan sat a few rows back with their families, wedged between cousins and aunts. I looked back at my brother-in-law's body, surrounded by flowers and wreaths.

"This is one of the four noble truths of the Buddha: life involves suffering. But that's not the way we think, is it? We think that life should be easy. We complain about our hardships. The weather. The president. The line at the grocery store.

"But today is truly difficult. Today we suffer because . . ." I took a breath to steady myself. ". . . because Joel is no longer with us."

I took a sip of water to hold it together. "Why do we never say these things?" I asked. "I've never heard a eulogy where someone just comes out and says, 'This is really difficult.' It's always words of comfort. But isn't it the greatest comfort to know that we are not alone, that we all suffer together?

"Today is a change," I continued, "and change is also difficult.

Consider the caterpillar morphing into a butterfly. Think about that for a second. It's a worm with legs, folks. And it turns into this delicate winged angel. You go from bird food to the cover of *Nature* magazine. Do you think that's easy? Wrapped in that cocoon, mutating its body? Got to be difficult.

"The snake shedding its skin. The tree adding to itself layer by layer. The universe expanding. How could these things be easy? They must involve great struggle. They must be difficult.

"Saint Paul, in his letter to the Romans, said, 'I do the things I don't want to do, and I don't want to do the things I do.' Or something like that. You didn't get a real pastor today; you got me."

No laughs, but a few smiles.

"Paul's point is that we all struggle. We struggle to do the right things, and we struggle to avoid the wrong things. The struggle is what makes us human. It is that struggle that gives us dignity, and worth, and self-respect. Today we honor those qualities in Joel.

"Talking with you all, I've heard the ways in which Joel's humanity—the person that he was beneath the struggles—touched our family and, in his own way, made the world a better place.

"My question for you today is: Can we struggle well? Can we struggle as Joel did? Can we struggle with this loss, accepting its difficulty but still embracing it? Can we look death in the face?" I paused, my emotions pushing for release.

"Because if we can struggle well, my friends, that is a life worth living." I turned to face Joel. "Just as Joel's was a life worth living."

I held it together for the rest of the service, until the final viewing. Over those cheap funeral home speakers came the voice of Johnny Cash singing his version of the Beatles classic "In My Life." And not a *young* Johnny Cash; this was the timeworn, weather-beaten Johnny Cash.

As people silently filed past to pay their final respects, Jade and I broke down in each other's arms.

CHAPTER 30

This Too Shall Pass

"I appreciate you seeing me, Martin." We were back in my old adviser's office, fish tank and frizzy hair where I left them.

"Anytime." Martin looked at me with concern, steeping his tea bag thoughtfully. "So things are not going well."

"I tried to zig when everyone else was zagging," I began. "Just like you said."

"Well, I didn't say it was going to be easy."

"This is such a grind, Martin." My eyes started to brim again.

"Then keep grinding."

"You don't understand." A tear rolled down my cheek. "I went from sixty-hour weeks to eighty-hour weeks. I'm losing sleep. My hair is falling out."

"*I* don't understand?" he said incredulously. "You really think *I* don't understand? Listen." He fished his tea bag out of his mug and set it on a ceramic tea bag holder. "Repeat after me. The four most important words in the entrepreneur's vocabulary: 'This too shall pass.'"

"This too shall pass," I mumbled.

"*THIS. TOO. SHALL. PASS.*"

"This too shall pass."

"Everything is temporary. All this"—he gestured toward the bookshelves, the awards, the trophy CEO photos—"shall pass. The good times as well as the bad. Endure. This, too, shall pass."

I grabbed a tissue and blew my nose. "How can you give so much of yourself and get so little in return?"

"It isn't over until you give up. It's *never* over until you give up." His frizz bobbed at me expectantly.

"You ever read *Man's Search for Meaning*?" he continued. "Viktor Frankl?"

"In college."

"He's this Jewish psychologist, remember, and he's sent to the Nazi death camps. Everything is taken from him—his work, his wealth, his family—and he just endures the most horrific things. He struggles to survive, to find meaning in this suffering, and he watches some of his fellow inmates just give up. He describes it like a light leaving their eyes. And within three days, they die."

"And the lesson is?"

"It's not over until you give up."

"That does put things in perspective." I smiled.

"Look, your goal was to run a billion-dollar company. And instead, you find yourself . . ."

"A billion dollars in debt?"

He laughed. "You can exaggerate your problems all you want, but good entrepreneurs just *make it happen*." He pointed the words. "You need the money? *Make it happen*. You need people to understand blockchain? *Make it happen*.

"Sometimes we give it everything, and it looks like we're getting nothing," he went on, putting his hand up at an angle. "But remember . . ."

"Please do not say 'hockey stick,'" I begged him.

"The *beginning* of the hockey stick," he corrected me. "Looks like you're not making any progress at all. Then . . ." He slowly tilted his hand into a forty-five-degree angle, then fifty degrees, then seventy-five . . .

Martin leaned in and lowered his voice. "The secret is really very simple."

"What's that?"

"*Bend the universe to your will.*"

SUMMARY

Let's wrap up the lessons in Part 3, so you can be ready to be reborn in Part 4.

+ **The market is unpredictable.** Like the stock market, the blockchain market is volatile—even more so as it goes through its moody teenage years.

+ **Reinventing industries.** Some of the most exciting projects in blockchain involve:

    + **Identity:** keeping our private information private, giving us better control over who can access it (like medical records).

    + **Two-party payments:** Holding money in "escrow" until both parties are satisfied with the job.

    + **Arbitration:** making it easier for parties to resolve differences without taking each other to court.

    + **Reward points:** creating a worldwide marketplace to buy and sell everything from frequent flyer miles to credit card points.

+ **Voting:** making transparent election systems that are of the people, by the people, and for the people.

+ **Blockchains are not companies.** While many of the rules of investing still apply, the blockchain itself is a new type of asset.

+ **Steady-drip investing.** The best way of protecting you from yourself is to set aside a monthly amount for investing into a balanced portfolio, preferably on auto-withdrawal. (More on this in Part 4.)

+ **"Picks and shovels" (and everything else).** There are plenty of blockchain investing opportunities in the traditional stock market.

  + **Mining hardware:** companies making the high-end computers and cards that "mine," or contribute to, a distributed blockchain network.

  + **Infrastructure:** traditional tech companies building out real blockchain expertise (not just paying lip service).

  + **Consulting:** traditional consulting firms creating a blockchain talent stack. (Quick test: See if they're publishing quality thought leadership about blockchain.)

  + **Patents:** companies staking their claim early, by filing patents around blockchain technology.

✦ **Financial services:** traditional financial companies and banks developing real blockchain applications (not just using blockchain as a buzzword).

✦ **Investor education.** The biggest need is to educate ordinary people on how to invest wisely. (Get ready for Part 4.)

REBIRTH

CHAPTER 31

Ending the Beginning

Paul Allen died.

I remember clearly where I received the text, because I was standing on Paul Allen's campus.

I was at Microsoft headquarters on an unseasonably warm day in early fall, with liquid sun pouring between the hemlocks and firs. Microsofties were jogging, playing soccer, hiking the five-hundred-acre wonderland.

I literally could not imagine a more beautiful place to work. Compared to our soggy coffee shop, this was ridiculously idyllic. Ridiculidyllic.

And Paul Allen built it.

This genius who cofounded Microsoft with Bill Gates, who built a multibillion-dollar investment portfolio, who gave away billions to charity, who was a benefactor to the city of Seattle, was gone. Today the weather in Redmond, where it always rains, seemed to be celebrating his life.

Allen's death was heavy on my mind as I prepared to take the stage at

Microsoft. He was a personal hero, and it was bizarre that I was speaking on the day of his passing. The coincidence felt pregnant with meaning, but like so many things in my life nowadays, I couldn't put my finger on why.

> Should I mention Paul Allen in my talk?

>> Definitely do not mention Paul Allen.

> Why not?

>> You don't even work there.

> Can I lead everyone in prayer?

> A prayer for Paul Allen?

> I'm serious.

As I texted Jade, a dynamic speaker named Peter Relan, the CEO of a new company called Got-It.ai, was onstage. Peter pitched the story of his company with the good humor and easy grace of a serial entrepreneur. It was intimidating: this was the major leagues, and he was a major-league pitcher.

"You need anything?" My two young Microsoft hosts, Matthew and Bruce, startled me from my anxious reverie.

"Another ten years of experience," I responded, nodding to Peter on the stage.

"He's great, isn't he?" Matthew smiled.

"Most blockchain speakers have the personality of oatmeal." As if on cue, the crowd laughed at one of Peter's jokes. "This guy is a superstar."

"You'll do fine," Matthew reassured me. "You got this."

"Hey, should I mention Paul Allen? Like, a moment of silence or something?"

Bruce frowned. "I wouldn't."

I pursed my lips. "Little problem, then."

"What do you need?" Matthew pointed to the stage, where Peter was walking off to huge applause. "Quickly. You're up."

I adjusted my headset and took a deep breath. "My whole talk was about Paul Allen."

The event was the Microsoft Gig Summit, where the subject was the "gig economy," the trend toward hiring freelance workers to drive you places (Uber), do graphic design (Upwork), or pick up your dry cleaning (TaskRabbit).

This was hardly a lunchroom training session: this was an employee *event*, held in a corporate theater with a full sound and lighting crew, professional photographers, and a lunch spread that included lobster sliders and hand-cut potato chips drizzled with truffle oil.

Mine was the last talk of the day, and I saw a number of Microsoft employees streaming for the exit as I took the stage. This threw me. I thought I was the closer, but now I saw I was the only thing standing between the audience and beating rush hour.

"Welcome to the last session of the day!" I began. "I'm John Hargrave . . ." And then I astrally projected toward the ceiling. *How am I going to introduce myself? Writer? Entrepreneur? Blockchain evangelist?*

Who am I?

I was looking down on my body, which was somehow talking to the crowd. It was surreal: the mouth was deciding what to say, but I was only dimly aware of the words coming out.

It was like going into a job interview and hearing the dreaded question "So tell me a little about yourself." It's not even a question! *What do you want to hear? Who do you want me to be? Which highlight reel from a lifetime of experiences do you want me to show?*

How do you position yourself as someone trustworthy, and interesting, and knowledgeable, and funny, and wise, all at the same time? We each have a collection of masks, different personas that we step into with family, friends, business colleagues, and so on. *Which mask should I wear?*

But the goal is to wear no mask. Isn't that what everyone says? "Just be yourself." What does that even mean? The goal is to be authentic. Which brought me back to my original question: *Who am I?*

I have no memory of what my mouth said for my introduction. I was out of body, all this spinning through my head, until I snapped back for the beginning of my presentation. Paul Allen was dead.

"Jack Ma can't buy the Internet," I improvised.

Blockchain Is Decentralized

Jack Ma is the richest man in China. He's so wealthy that some Chinese households keep his picture in their home, sitting alongside a picture of Caishen, the Chinese god of prosperity. He's a modern-day deity. He's not just a billionaire, he's a bill*yuan*aire.[53]

Ma is so rich that on any given day, he could literally buy all the tea in China.[54]

Even with all this wealth, Jack Ma cannot buy the Internet. The very idea seems kind of silly. We all know the Internet is a huge network of computers, and no one owns it. There's no Internet headquarters, no Internet CEO, no Internet power cord that someone could unplug.

That's because the Internet is **decentralized**.

Our brains are not wired for decentralization. First, it's six syllables, which is overwhelming. Second, most of the human institutions we've built are centralized. Governments, churches, Microsoft. For hundreds of years we've been building nation-states, with centralized capitals, leaders, and institutions.

Which is not to say that centralized institutions are bad.

In fact, many of today's issues are the result of friction between centralization and decentralization: the role of a centralized media in a decentralized social media world, for example. Or how a centralized military responds to decentralized terrorist networks.

Blockchain has decentralization in its DNA. Bitcoin, for example, is not a company. There's

> **Decentralized:** not owned or controlled by a central institution. The most useful example is the Internet.
>
> Be wary of "private" or "permissioned" blockchains, which are more centralized. Ask: *Why do they need blockchain?*
>
> KEY TERM

no president of Ethereum. Blockchains may have foundations or consortiums—in the same way the Internet has a standards-setting body—but they are generally not run by a guy behind a mahogany desk.

This is counterintuitive. To say "Let's create this massive blockchain project, then give it away to the world" is in direct opposition to the American Dream: Work hard, believe in yourself, build a big company, then sell it for a profit.

I'm not saying that blockchain entrepreneurs are Mother Teresas.

But the more they focus on building useful technology, the more it seems they profit in spite of themselves. Their wealth seems almost like a blockchain by-product.

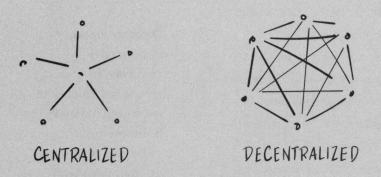

CENTRALIZED   DECENTRALIZED

The best example of decentralization is how a humble black-smith changed the course of history. We owe much of our modern-day society to this lone horseshoe-smelting genius.

That blacksmith was named Johannes Gutenberg, who in the 1400s remixed several existing technologies—such as woodblock printing and screw presses for making wine—to create the first printing press.

This humble invention set off a chain reaction of social good: suddenly knowledge—information—was within reach of everyone. Before the printing press, if you wanted to hear the Bible, you had to go to church and listen to it read by priests. Now: Bibles for everyone!

Humans, it turns out, love to learn. The more information, the better! Printing presses started churning out volumes as fast as their screw presses would allow, creating a knowledge snowball. More books led to more ideas, which led to more literacy, which led to even more books and more ideas.

As the snowball picked up speed, it led to the Reformation,

the Scientific Revolution, and the Industrial Revolution—as the old heads of state and church were gradually displaced by the new ideas. By 1500, there were twenty million books; by the next century, there were two hundred million.[55]

If this sounds familiar, that's because it's just like blockchain.

Imagine if Gutenberg had said, "This is a great invention. I will patent it. Then I will print a small collection of books on blacksmithing. My first work will be a memoir called *Hammering It Home*. The second will be a treasured volume of blacksmith jokes called *He Who Smelt It*."

If Gutenberg had centralized his knowledge—if he had kept the printing press to himself—we might have ended up with the Gutenberg Booklets instead of the Gutenberg Bible. But the printing press was a decentralized *invention* that decentralized *information*.

When we cast our bread upon the waters, we may end up with a soggy bagel—but when we put good things into the world, they seem to come back to us multiplied.

I'm building something that I won't own. That's the mind shift that's so hard for companies and governments and central banks to understand. But if you don't build open blockchains, then someone else will. Then you've lost your seat at the table. You're a passenger, not a driver.

Look at Hyperledger, the blockchain platform started by the Linux Foundation (itself a centralized organization that works on the decentralized Linux). Hyperledger is a decentralized project backed by a consortium of centralized technology companies like IBM and Cisco.

Centralized organizations can work on decentralized blockchains; they just can't "own" them in the traditional sense. And that's scary. "How are we going to make money from this?" the boss will ask. "What's in it for us?" our politicians will wonder.

But these are the same questions asked throughout the history of disruptive technologies.

"Why should we be interested in printing?" asked the Catholic Church of the 1400s. "We've been copying Bibles by hand for almost fourteen hundred years." Meanwhile, the people were now reading their own Bibles, coming up with their own interpretations, and deciding the Church needed a reformation.

"Why should we be interested in the Internet?" asked the media companies of the 1990s. "We've been printing books, magazines, and newspapers for hundreds of years." Meanwhile, the Internet was making it easier than ever to publish, copy, and print, mowing down the media landscape.

Just like the Internet, no one can own the blockchain—though many companies and governments will try. Be wary of "private" blockchains, which are for the private good, and do not confuse them with "public" blockchains, which are for the public good.

The paradox of the Internet is that no one owns it, but everyone owns it. It's decentralized. Look for blockchains that are decentralized.

"Today's event is about the gig economy," I concluded, "which is a form of decentralization. You don't own gig workers. In fact, the gig workers own you. You rely on them to run your business.

"Decentralization is radical!" I shouted, startling a young woman in the second row. "Decentralization is going to disrupt everything you do at Microsoft, so get this model in your head."

I began fishing for examples. "The Internet service in Cuba is terrible, so the citizens built their own version called SNET, short for 'street network.' Everyone connects their computers, and a community of volunteers provides technical support. The people own SNET, and the government looks the other way as long as they behave. That's decentralization." A few geeks nodded their heads. *Mesh networks.*

"Or remember, as a child, when you'd get together with your friends and put on a little play for the grown-ups? That was decentralization. No one owned it. You *all* owned it.

"Potluck dinners. Spontaneous gatherings. Memes. Slang. The spread of a good idea. These are all examples of decentralization, and decentralization is the spirit of blockchain."

I hesitated: now came the controversial part.

"And when you are decentralizing into a gig economy," I went on, "you must remember that *gig workers are people*." I clicked to my next slide: a typical photo of ethnically diverse smiling people. "Not these people," I clarified. "This is a stock photo." Some laughs.

"Look: I am stunned by the beauty of your campus. But remember that gig workers don't work in this environment. They're working from coffee shops, in the pouring rain. They're freelancing from home, with screaming children in the background. They're constantly hustling for their next gig. It's a grind.

"The temptation for all of us is to treat gig workers as expendable, as faceless cogs in a digital factory. But these are human beings. The more you treat them as human beings, the more they will reward you in kind." One or two gig workers in the back of the theater clapped, sending a thrill up my spine.

"Even the great Paul Allen couldn't have bought the Internet," I concluded, "God rest his soul. No one owns the Internet, yet we all own it. Blockchain is the same way. It belongs to the people. Power to the people. Blockchain for everyone."

Backstage, I worried. The applause had been so-so, not the revolution I was hoping to incite. It had been a long day, and I think everyone wanted to get home. Matthew and Bruce were still full of energy, though.

"Hey, I brought you a gift," Bruce blurted out, handing me a book.

I looked at the cover. *Tao of Jeet Kune Do* by Bruce Lee. "Interesting." I thumbed through the pages. "Should I read it now, or . . . ?"

"No," he laughed. "I read your book *Mind Hacking*, and I think a lot of Bruce Lee's philosophies are similar to yours. I thought you'd enjoy it."

"Thanks for the Bruce, Bruce." I thumbed through the pages, a collection of Lee's signature martial arts moves interspersed with his philosophy of Zen. I landed on:

"He wrote down these sayings in a little notebook he carried around with him," Bruce explained. "Kind of like affirmations. Mind hacks."

"Mind hacks," I marveled. "In a notebook."

Peter, the dynamic entrepreneur from earlier, walked over and shook my hand. "I'm really interested in blockchain," he told me, "but my current company is more focused on AI." He had a youthful exuberance that belied his age; I could picture him running a spiritual retreat. "I liked your story about that woman shocking you in your booth."

"Painful memory." I smiled.

"So you guys still do your content agency work, right? We're growing like crazy, and we could use your help. It's AI, not blockchain . . . at least, not yet." He looked at me meaningfully.

"We would love to help," I replied, inwardly breathing a sigh of relief.

"Great. Let's talk next week." He handed me a card and disappeared out the door.

"Well, *that* was worth the trip," Matthew commented.

"You have no idea," I replied. The plane was grazing the tops of trees, headed for a mountain. This was a little more gas in the tank, maybe just enough to clear the mountain.

Paul Allen might be dead, but we would live to see another day!

CHAPTER 32

Tearing It Up

Media Shower was down to a skeleton crew.

As the price of bitcoin continued to drop—it had plunged below $5,000—the blockchain business began to dry up. The media began to call it "Crypto Winter," and I frequently stayed awake long into the night, wondering how we were going to survive until the spring thaw.

If it seemed otherwise, it's because I was speaking at more and more conferences—but always for free. I had even upgraded my wardrobe and hired a booking agent, but none of the blockchain conferences wanted to pay. It was another example of "pay to play": most speakers were hyping their blockchain projects, so they had to pay their own way. But, like a struggling standup comedian, I worked for free.

It gave me a lot of opportunity to work out new material. Today I was at a large blockchain conference at Boston's World Trade Center, where I was addressing a function room filled with blockchain investors.

"If blockchain really is a new asset class," I began after warming up the crowd, "then how do we value them? How do we measure them?"

I clicked to the same stock photo of ethnically diverse smiling people that I had used at Microsoft.

"I remind you that the blockchain is about people. You have to get people using the damn things. Blockchain is powered by the people. Power to the people!" I had taken to raising my hand in a fist, which my wife told me looked like I was trying to lead a geek power rally.

"Power to the people," I repeated, awkwardly lowering my hand. "And if this technology really is about people," I soldiered on, "then we need a metric to measure people using a blockchain.

"And that leads us to the one metric that matters, the one rule to rule them all. We call it the *Rocket Rule*."

Network Effects: The Rocket Rule

Did you ever wonder who owned the first telephone?

Alexander Graham Bell, obviously, but I mean the first telephone after *that*. I want to hear Bell's pitch. "Why, take a gander at this amazing device that allows you to speak, using your ordinary voice, to any other human being, *regardless of location!*"

Network effects: For each new person that joins a network, the network becomes more useful for everyone. Good examples are the telephone and Facebook.

"Really?" asks his prospective customer, who certainly has a handlebar mustache and jaunty bowler hat. "Who else owns one?"

"Well, just me."

"Right. So I can only talk to you."

"Yes." Bell looks deflated. "And Mrs. Bell, too."

BIG DEAL

"Oh!" Bowler Hat perks up. "*Mrs. Bell? Sign me up!*" he exclaims, and dozens of other eager gentlemen get in line to place their orders.

This produces what we call **network effects**, and the classic example is the telephone. When only Mr. and Mrs. Bell owned a telephone, there was just one connection. When five people joined, there were ten possible connections, and with twelve people there were sixty-six connections.

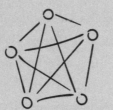 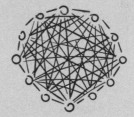

2 USERS = 1 CONNECTION   5 USERS = 10 CONNECTIONS   12 USERS = 66 CONNECTIONS

The more people who get a phone, the more useful the phone becomes for everyone.

Most modern technologies leverage network effects in some way. Facebook started as a small network at Harvard, then expanded to other Ivy League schools, then expanded to all schools, then expanded to all grandmothers. As more people joined, Facebook became more useful for all people.

Blockchains enjoy network effects big-time. In other words, the more users you get on your blockchain, the more useful the blockchain becomes for all users. The more people who own bitcoin, for example, the more useful it becomes to buy, sell, or trade.

Network effects are quantified in a mathematical equation known as **Metcalfe's law**, named after Internet pioneer Bob Metcalfe. Simply put, the value of a network grows proportionally to the square of the number of users *n*:

$$value_{blockchain} = \frac{n\,(n-1)}{2}$$

where *n* = number of users

Metcalfe's law (which is more a rule of thumb than a law) has been shown to describe the value of publicly traded "network" companies like Facebook and Tencent.[56] It has been used to describe the Internet itself.[57] It is why traditional investors value "network effect" companies so highly.

The term to use is not "*exponential* growth" but "*quadratic* growth." Here's the easy way to explain it: every time we double the number of users, we increase the number of connections 4x. Here's what the value of Bell's telephone network looks like as he sells his first ten telephones:

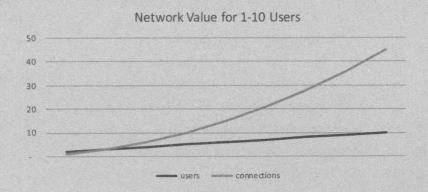

In other words, with ten users, each user has fifty possible telephone connections. Now let's imagine an investor came along and said, "See here, Mr. Bell. I'll pay you $50 to buy this newfangled tele-phonium network of yours." Bell now has a valuation of $5 per user ($50 ÷ 10), or $1 per connection.

What a deal for Mr. Bell! Armed with this initial valuation of $1 per connection, watch how the value of the overall network grows as we go from ten to one hundred users:

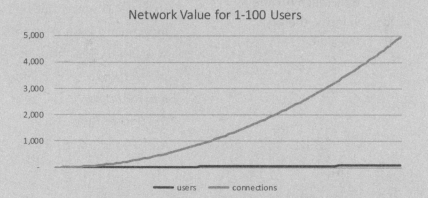

Network Value for 1-100 Users

Our brains are not wired to think this way. We are accustomed to linear growth, because it's how we experience most things in everyday life: we age at a linear rate; prices go up in a slow but linear fashion; we get linear increases in pay.

Imagine a bus that accelerates not linearly but quadratically: the driver steps on the gas, and it goes from 1 to 3 to 6 to 10 miles per hour. *Man, this bus takes a while to get going,* you think as it accelerates from 15 to 21 to 28 to 36 miles per hour. A line of cars is backed up behind the Blockchain Bus, honking impatiently.

Then it jumps to 45, then 55, then 66, then 78, then 91, then 105 miles per hour. You are still giving it the same amount of gas, but it's accelerating to 120, 136, 153, 171, 190, and 210 miles per hour. Soon passengers are holding on for dear life as a nose cone of

Rocket Rule: As blockchains attract initial users, they lift off slowly, following Metcalfe's law. Once they reach escape velocity, the sky's the limit.

BIG DEAL

fire envelops the front of the bus, heat friction tearing panels off the sides.

Quadratic growth is like a rocket taking off: At first, it looks like nothing is happening. A lot of smoke and noise, but no movement. By the time you realize you have liftoff, the rocket is heading into orbit. We'll call this the **Rocket Rule**.

After my opening remarks, I was scheduled to do an onstage interview with one of Boston's leading blockchain investors. I sat down in the chair next to him, giving him a once-over. Jeans, blazer, designer glasses. Full head of hair. "Finn, you're starting a venture capital firm using blockchain," I threw it to him. "Tell us how it works."

"Sure. In the traditional VC structure," he explained, "you have a small number of limited partners who put in capital."

"They give you their money to invest," I translated, "which you, the VC company, invest in new startups."

"Exactly."

" 'Venture' means new business; 'capital' means money. 'Venture capital' means money for new businesses."

He eyed me suspiciously. "Thank you."

"I was up all night reading *Venture Capital for Dummies*," I joked. It wasn't a joke.

"Can I finish?"

"Please."

"With our new tokenized VC firm, anyone will be able to invest, get in on the ground floor of these new investing opportunities—"

"Let's unpack this," I interrupted again. "Let's say you guys find the next Facebook. Now everyone who owns your token will be rewarded, because the value of the token will skyrocket."

"It really lets everyone get in on the ground floor."

"And by 'everyone,' you mean everyone?" I clarified.

"Well, accredited investors living in the United States."

"So the wealthy."

"Well, that's almost 10 percent of households in America," he came back.[58]

"So the kinda wealthy."

"Well, that's the way the securities laws are written," he explained.

I sat silently for a moment, my blood beginning to boil. Man, there's nothing like a well-placed silence to really get an audience's attention. I stretched out that silence until something snapped.

Yes, and . . .

"That's the way the securities laws are written," I repeated. "Yes, and the way the securities laws are written is out of date and out of touch. You know what?" I ripped up my page of notes and dropped them theatrically to the floor. "You know the two words I never want to hear again? 'Accredited investor.' We should *all* be accredited investors."

Applause from the audience. Finally, after a year of drilling, I had struck pay dirt.

"Blockchain is a decentralized movement," I ranted, "by the people, for the people, of the people. But the people are sitting on the sidelines, timid and afraid, waiting for the government to tell them what to do! *We want Daddy to tell us what to do.*"

"Look, our job is to make sure we're compliant with all *existing* securities laws," the VC answered coolly. "If you want to change those laws, if you don't think they're ideal . . . well, I don't disagree."

"So you agree," I fired back.

He looked like I had spat a mouthful of goldfish water at him.

"If you don't disagree, then you agree," I clarified.

He blinked, unsure what he was agreeing with. Normally these blockchain interviews were as dry as toast. A few people in the audience were wide-eyed and grinning, unsure whether they were allowed to laugh.

"Why make everything so complicated?" I asked. "Why not just say that anyone can invest in blockchain tokens? Level the playing field once and for all?"

"Well, our existing securities laws were written in the 1930s," he replied, "and were meant to protect investors from gambling away their life savings."

"Then we have to restrict gambling to the wealthy as well. No more casinos, no more lottery tickets, no more scratch cards, unless you're an accredited investor. You can't have it both ways." A few brave souls applauded.

"So you want to lead a revolution—"

"We *all* want to lead a revolution," I interrupted. "We the people. That's what it means. *We* are the people. The government serves *us*. They have their power by *our* authority. In times when our government fails us, then—like the shareholders of a mismanaged company—*we* must lead. We must self-organize. That is what blockchain allows us to do."

"I was wondering when we'd get around to blockchain again," Finn quipped, and got a big laugh.

"We've got to lead," I carried on. "You think the government understands this stuff? They're a million miles up, man! *We've* got to write the vision for the future, or the future will be written for us. Old boss, same as the new boss." The wheels were falling off my bus. "I mean, new boss, same as . . . ah, shoot."

"You were doing so well," he remarked.

"Can I get an amen?" I called. I did not get an amen.

"We agree that blockchain can change our systems of finance, government, business," Finn saved me. "And these are powerful systems. They resist change. New technologies always threaten the status quo, and often disrupt the incumbent."

"You mean they force the people in power to change," I translated. "Evolve or die."

"Yes, and you're right that we must lead. We're trying to do our part by opening up venture capital a little wider. Step by step. Slow and steady wins the race."

"Evolution, not revolution."

"*You* say you want a revolution." He smiled.

"Everyone together!" I spontaneously led audience in song—and *some of them actually sang along.*

You say you want a revolution
We all wanna change the world . . .

Now came the awkward part: meeting up with Finn backstage.

I had all these things I wanted to say. *This stuff matters, and I'm just trying to make it interesting so people will care. I'm taking an extreme position to make a point. I cannot match your power and wealth, but I now know how to talk your language. I have infiltrated your system.*

"Thanks for the great interview," was all I said.

"Are you kidding? That was possibly the greatest interview I've done at one of these conferences," he laughed. "We really had each other on the ropes!"

"Well, I had *you* on the ropes," I corrected him.

"I was a theater major in college," he confided, "and the stage is actually my one true love."

"Really?" I tried to picture him as Hamlet.

"Really. That was great theater. I get it."

"You get it." Dumbfounded.

"Listen, we're having a big investor meeting next month. Not like this." He waved dismissively around him. "*Real* investors. Family offices, institutions. I'd love for you to emcee."

"You want me to emcee?"

"We've got to make this stuff interesting," he told me.

"We've got to make this stuff interesting."

"I'll have my team set it up with you." We shook hands. "Now, we have a limited budget. But we'll wine and dine you along with the investors. It'll be great networking, great exposure."

I was so surprised, I didn't even register that he had just gotten me to agree to do it for free. "Where is the event?" I asked.

"The Ritz-Carlton."

Limited budget!

I left the conference walking on air. Something in me had been unlocked. Another unpaid gig, but, hey, dinner at the Ritz-Carlton with some millionaires didn't sound so shabby.

I thought back to the Rocket Rule: For a long time it looks like nothing's happening. Then, before you know it, the rocket has reached escape velocity and is heading into orbit.

But it was so hard to *know*. Business was still so bad. Would we reach orbit? Or would the rocket break up under the pressure?

CHAPTER 33

Crazy Rich Asians

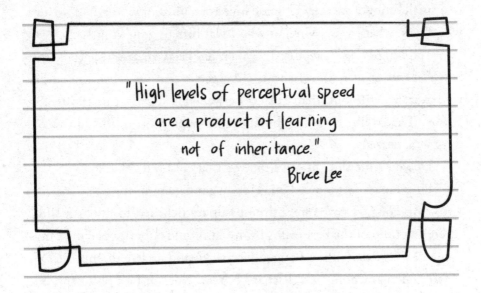

"High levels of perceptual speed
are a product of learning
not of inheritance."

Bruce Lee

There was no Ping-Pong table.

This bummed me out. I was at the Massachusetts Institute of Technology: the tech capital of the world! Nerd-vana! There had to be n Ping-Pong tables within radius r, but I could not solve for n.

First there was me trying to explain to my Chinese host why I needed a Ping-Pong table to talk about blockchain. Then trying to squeeze my own Ping-Pong table into my tiny electric car. Getting quotes for Ping-Pong table delivery. I had been practicing for weeks! But

Ping-Pong is a game of finesse, not force. Accepting defeat, I prepared a Ping-Pong video instead.

"I want to begin today," I began, "by talking about Ping-Pong."

I was speaking to the Boston Chinese Investment Club, a group born out of the MIT Sloan School of Management, a school that had minted its fair share of tech millionaires. Blockchain investing was all the rage in China, all the more so because Initial Coin Offerings (ICOs) had recently been banned by the Chinese government.

Now all the money was moving to Hong Kong—and to the United States. Which was why I was standing in a lecture hall at MIT, speaking to a small room of wealthy Chinese investors, most of whom had no idea who I was, what I was saying, or why I was bringing up Ping-Pong.

"Yes, Ping-Pong," I repeated. "Much has been made of the trade war between our great nations, and the danger is that we fall into another cold war like the one that existed between us during the 1950s and 1960s." I acted like I was in China, even though most of these investors were U.S. citizens.

"Do you remember how we thawed that cold war?" I asked.

"Ping-Pong!" announced one elderly gentleman in the back.

"Ping-Pong." I gave him a thumbs-up and clicked to my next slide. "Here's a photo of the best teams from China and America playing Ping-Pong. We called it 'Ping-Pong diplomacy,' and it led to this." *Click*. "Mao Zedong meeting with Richard Nixon. Not our best president, but not our worst." Easy laugh.

"How many of you know this man?" I asked, advancing another slide. A hand went up. "Who is it?"

"Ma Long," replied a well-dressed woman.

"Ma Long!" I shouted, startling even myself. "During the 2016 Summer Olympics, my brother and I watched the great Chinese table tennis player Ma Long with a mixture of fascination and awe. Absolute fanboys. And when he would score a point on a forearm power smash, we would go like this."

I cupped my hands to my mouth. "MAAAAAAA LOOOOOONG!"

They may have been crazy rich Asians, but they were looking at me regular crazy.

"Watch this," I said, and pulled up the YouTube video. It shows Ma Long facing off against Japan's world champion, Jun Mizutani. The volleys grow more and more frenetic, with both opponents several feet from the table, swinging their paddles full force, the ball a blur. Then Ma Long goes in for a final return, checks himself, and the ball misses the table by inches. *Ma Long's point.* The crowd on the video goes berserk, and even in the room people caught their breath.

"Come on!" I told the crowd, cupping my mouth. "MAAAAAAAA LOOOOOOOOONG!"

And they did it! *They actually did the Ma Long chant.*

"My point is that competition can be fun. It can be a game. Our politicians talk about trade wars, but a game is the opposite of a war. A game is something we play together." Then I told the story about Lester.

Listening to Lester

I live in a small town outside Boston that has given me a taste of direct democracy in the form of town meetings. These are regular meetings, held since our town was founded in the 1600s, where the townspeople meet to vote on policy and budgets.

Direct democracy, I have learned, is hard work. There's one older gentleman—I'll call him Lester—who has opinions on every topic imaginable. At one town meeting, there was discussion on what the animal control department should do about the gophers.

Old Lester shuffled up to the microphone. Everyone can speak for three minutes, and Lester never misses an opportunity. "Gophers are evil!" he proclaimed. "They dig up your yard, chew up your grass, they mate and lay their babies in your holes. *Get yourself a shotgun!*"

Lester's rant on gophers went on for the full three minutes.

Another town meeting focused on the highway department. (There's no highway, and in fact only one stoplight.) Could the highway department cut down a large, rotting stump? A woman—I'll call her Dolores—fought for that stump as if it were a memorial to her dead husband.

"There is a family of *squirrels* living in that tree!" she cried, on the verge of tears. She called the stump a tree. "And those squirrels charm everyone who walks past!" I sat patiently, trying to recall ever being charmed by a squirrel, or indeed any rodent, ever.

The moderators of our town meetings have the patience of saints. After about a half hour of this, I start to go stir-crazy. I mean, I work on the Internet, where everyone wants to make a million dollars before lunch. Three minutes on gophers? Ninety minutes on stumps?

But that's what democracy is all about. When we say everybody gets a say, we mean *everybody*: not just the bright and articulate folks, but those who have a lot of time alone at home.

The dream of democracy is one person, one vote. But when you're actually in the dream, it can be kind of a nightmare. You see this playing out in the worldwide blockchain community today, and it's forking annoying.

———

Work It Out, Don't Fork It Out

Here's a real-life example. As bitcoin has grown in popularity, the bitcoin network runs too slowly and uses too much power, and it costs too much to make a transaction. It needs an upgrade, but what's the best path forward?

Here we have to rely on the core bitcoin developers, each of whom has his or her own solution to the problem. Typically these solutions are hashed out on Internet message boards (bad idea), which results in flame wars and BBC-miniseries-level drama.

Often one team's solution wins out, and the other team decides to go their own way, which results in a bitcoin **fork**. It's as if we made a copy of our accounting ledger, then started keeping two separate copies of the ledger at a certain point in time—parallel realities, if you will.

Real democracy is hard, and blockchain is a real democracy. The blockchain is about people, but many blockchain developers don't have the best people skills. It's easier to fork it out than to work it out. But united we stand; divided we fail.

Fork: when a blockchain is split into two different versions, like a fork in the road.

Bitcoin has been forked several times, resulting in altcoins designed for different uses: Bitcoin Cash, Bitcoin Gold, and Bitcoin Private, for example.

KEY TERM

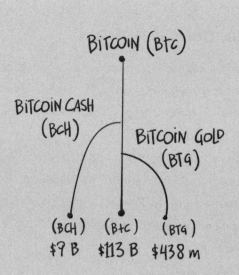

BITCOIN (BTC)

BITCOIN CASH (BCH)

BITCOIN GOLD (BTG)

(BCH) (BTC) (BTG)
$9 B $113 B $438 m

What's needed are better systems of governance, better forums of dialogue and debate. I picture a kind of United Nations of Blockchain, where leading developers meet to hash out problems with their hashing algorithms. Let's call them #HashOuts.

I see these as in-person meetings, modeled after town hall meetings in rural America, or citizens' meetings in Switzerland. There's a moderator. Everyone gets three minutes to speak. There are official votes. Ping-Pong tables should definitely be involved.

Governance: the system for managing changes to a blockchain project. Part of this is coded into the blockchain itself (like laws), but part of it depends on the people who oversee that system (like a government).

KEY TERM

If blockchain is so great at democracy, you might be thinking, *why can't you do all this on the blockchain?* For the same reason you can't set fiscal policy by consulting your accounting ledger. People need to play Ping-Pong.

Writing the code for blockchain is like writing the laws for a country. It takes all the planning, process, proposals, and the Ping-Pong of government. That's why we call this messy, wonderful process **governance**.

If we can figure out how to take the best processes of direct democracy and apply them to the blockchain itself, then it's possible that we—that is, we the people—can take over the world. More on that later.

Playing Ping-Pong is hard work. (Just ask Ma Long.) It requires patience and persistence. It requires that we listen to Lester.

A silver-haired investor raised his hand. "So you're basically saying to work together."

"Well, friendly competition can help us both get better," I replied. "The operative word is 'friendly.'"

"I think you're being awfully naive," he replied.

"Or hopeful." I smiled.

A well-dressed young woman raised her hand. "Now that China has banned ICOs," she said, "I'm wondering what you think about jurisdictional arbitrage."

"Juris—what? I'm sorry."

"Jurisdictional arbitrage."

"Still not getting it."

"Juris . . ."

This went on for an uncomfortably long time. Not the type of Ping-Pong I wanted.

Jurisdictional arbitrage. "Jurisdiction" = territory, location. "Arbitrage" = exploiting price discrepancies. Exploiting price discrepancies between territories?

"I think we're seeing the money move to other territories," I vamped, trying to stall while I figured it out. "The investment dollars are going to other regions." Now I was just saying words. "Hong Kong. South Korea." Now I was just reciting countries in Asia. "North Korea."

I should have just said, "I have no idea what that question means," I thought. *Why am I so afraid to admit what I don't know?* Silently I vowed not to make this mistake again.

"Exactly," she said. At least one of us was satisfied. "The blockchain economy is global."

"Traded twenty-four hours a day, all over the world," I agreed. "Blockchain never sleeps."

"But if you want to invest in blockchain and your country bans it, what do you do?"

"You can move somewhere else." A few chuckles. "There are forward-thinking governments creating blockchain-friendly environments to attract investors and entrepreneurs. There's even a big blockchain community in Puerto Rico, which uses U.S. money, but better for taxes."

Jurisdictional arbitrage! Like when Apple opened a big office in Ireland to take advantage of friendlier tax laws. That's what she meant! "Jurisdictional arbitrage," I wrapped up, pointing at her.

MAAAAAAA LOOOOOOOOOOOOOOONG! I thought to myself, thinking I had just completed the equivalent of the forearm power smash. Only later would I learn that Asians find it rude to point your finger at someone.

"Thank you for your questions, and thank you for your time," I concluded, giving a little bow. There was polite applause, and I unhooked my laptop for the next speaker, who had already approached the podium and was standing in front of me.

I smiled politely and tried to remove my video adapter, but it was stuck to the HDMI cable. The room had grown deathly silent. Time slowed down as I wriggled it free.

My clicker was still in my hand. I put it back in its protective sleeve, which took fifteen minutes. The next speaker was waiting, smiling, nodding. I was fumbling with my mouse, putting it back in my bag. *Why did I have so many peripherals?* Did I also bring a printer?

Meanwhile, pure silence. No one on laptops. No one on phones. Everyone politely waiting, smiling, nodding. Ages passed. My kids graduated college.

Now my laptop went back in the bag, like packing a box of heavy dishes to be shipped overseas. Bubble wrap. Labels. Now applying postage stamps, one by one. I died and was reincarnated as an ass.

Finally, I stepped down from the podium, packed up and ready to hike the Appalachian Trail. That's when I realized the gentleman was not the next speaker. He was waiting to present me with a thank-you gift. With two hands and a bow, he handed me a box containing a beautiful fountain pen featuring the Chinese flag. The audience applauded.

A few nights later I'd use this pen to sketch out an important realization.

CHAPTER 34

Metrics That Matter

"Sorry I'm late." I shook the rain off my coat. "It's miserable outside."

"Just getting started," said Kirk. "We're playing Gold Digger."

"How are things?" asked Evan, pulling up a chair.

"Like I'm running a marathon in that weather outside." I cracked open a seltzer. "With a ferret in my pants."

"This is blockchain?" Ben clarified.

"This is my life now," I sighed, sitting down.

"What's the latest bitcoin price?"

"Don't ask."

"You boys remember the rules," Kirk ran down. "We're staking claims on plots of land. Some are filled with gold, some with fool's gold, and some with both."

"I can't tell you how many new blockchain projects are backed by gold," I remarked.

"How many by fool's gold?" Ben asked.

"Did you know the U.S. government went off the gold standard to stop other countries from pillaging our gold supply?" Evan began riffing. "When the dollar was backed by gold, you could trade a million dollars for a million dollars' worth of gold. Other countries would just load up on dollars, then buy out our gold supply."

"The gold standard was a good idea." Ben laid down a token on a claim card. "The government could print more money only if it mined more gold. The money was backed by real value."

"So what backs up our money today?" Kirk asked, drawing a card.

"Trust," I replied, "like everything else. But the government can erode that trust if it keeps printing money."

"A lot of the blockchain projects I've checked out have that problem," Evan observed. "Even if they start out with some value, they reserve the right to mint more tokens, which devalues everyone's token."

"Please explain," Kirk asked.

The Parable of the Goldbuckians

Let's imagine two governments. One has a fixed quantity of currency backed by gold reserves, so every "Goldbuck" is redeemable for one ounce of gold. The other government has no gold and just prints "Airbucks" whenever it wants.

For blockchain investors, this concept is critical. Some tokens (like bitcoin) have a fixed supply programmed into their code. There are twenty-one million bitcoin, and there won't be any more. Period.

Other tokens have the ability to create more on demand. Let's say you own ten AirCoins out of one hundred total, or 10 percent of the AirCoin supply. The team behind AirCoin needs to raise money, so they create an additional nine hundred tokens and sell them at the going rate (which goes down as they sell them).

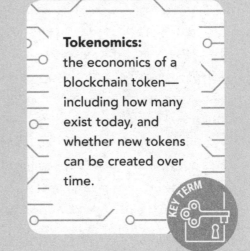

Tokenomics: the economics of a blockchain token— including how many exist today, and whether new tokens can be created over time.

Now you own ten out of one thousand total, or 1 percent of the total supply: they've "printed money," creating tokens out of thin air, and devalued your investment.

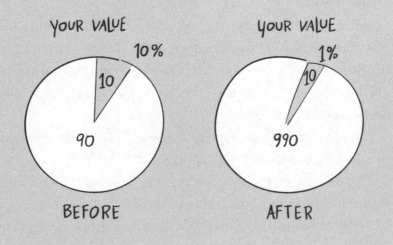

YOUR VALUE

10%
10
90

BEFORE

YOUR VALUE

1%
10
990

AFTER

Of course, this happens in real economies all the time. Governments are constantly printing money with nothing to back it up. There's no real value behind it except our collective belief that the new money is as good as the old money.

"But aren't *all* tokens created out of thin air?" a skeptic will ask. At first, yes. But once the value of that economy is established, any unexpected new tokens will "water down" the value of all tokens. It is for this reason that the rules of the economy—the "tokenomics"—are so important.

Tokenomics is an uncharted discipline, and there are very few best practices. If your kids are going into college, tell them to dual-major in economics and computer science. In the years to come, tokenomists are going to pull down some serious coin.

"That's just it," Ben cut in. "I still don't get the value in blockchain. I'm a value investor. Find great companies and buy them when their stock goes on sale."

"Stocks that are trading at a good value," I agreed, playing a card.

"A classic value company is, you know, Dairy Queen or Heinz. Good brands, good economics, and a good stock price. That's value."

"I'd say the value comes from the fact that we all *believe* it's valuable," I stated. "Look at Tesla."

"Ben just put down his deposit on a new Tesla," Kirk informed me.

I raised my eyebrows. "Congratulations."

"Thanks," Ben continued. "My point is, you've got to find some way of measuring the value of these blockchains."

"We're working on it," I moaned. "It's a hard problem. We know the blockchain is about people," I said for the hundredth time, "and the more people on a blockchain, the more valuable it becomes. Network effects."

"So why not just take the total value of a blockchain and divide it by the number of people using it?"

"It's complicated," I answered, staking a claim on a card. "Some blockchains are private. People can have multiple wallets."

"Just take the blockchain market as a whole," Wharton grad Evan suggested. He played the last card. "That's game."

I fished around in my rain-drenched coat for my Moleskine notebook and Chinese pen. Inspired, I quickly sketched out:

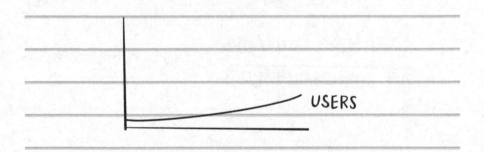

"Let's say the number of blockchain investors grows linearly," I said as Kirk counted up everyone's score. Then I sketched another line.

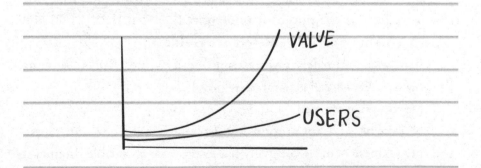

"The total value of all blockchains should increase like this." *Quadratic growth. Network effects.* "As more users come on board, the blockchain becomes more useful for all users. The Rocket Rule."

"That's interesting," Evan observed. "If there's a fixed number of tokens, each token will become more valuable because it's 'holding' more value in the network."

I thought for a moment. "The value comes from the people."

Of course!

It was like I unlocked a wild tiger in my head. I hurriedly wrote down:

$$\frac{\text{TOTAL BLOCKCHAIN VALUE}}{\text{TOTAL BLOCKCHAIN WALLETS}} = \text{VALUE PER PERSON}$$

That's it. That has to be it.

These would become our fundamentals for valuing the blockchain market. They could be used as "guardrails" to show whether the blockchain market was overpriced or underpriced—not perfectly, but close enough. (For more detail, see **Reference Guide 3**.)

"Ben, what ultimately gives a company its value? *People.* Revenue, profit, whatever—it's all generated by people."

"Maybe," Ben allowed.

"No maybe." I spun around my Moleskine notebook and tapped with my Chinese pen. "A company has to produce a valuable product to attract customers, but the customers in turn provide the value to the company. A blockchain must provide value for the people, but the people provide the value for the blockchain. *Measure the people and you measure the value.*"

"Well, guess who won the game," Kirk announced, looking at me.

CHAPTER 35

Chicken Fight

The Global Blockchain Summit wasn't global.

Also, it wasn't a summit.

When they asked me to speak (for free), the original venue had been a large amphitheater in Boston. The website showed gourmet food, hundreds of attendees, top business leaders from all over the world. How could I say no? This was the *Global Blockchain Summit*!

Now I stood inside the lobby of a tiny coworking space, peering into a glass-walled conference room of maybe a dozen people. In one corner a half-eaten pizza drooped sadly over the edge of its cardboard box, soggy salad strewn about the table.

Then I saw a face I recognized from the website: the speaker scheduled to go on before me. He was a prominent Harvard academic I was looking forward to hearing. We made eye contact as he approached. "Not worth my time," he muttered, walking out the door and onto the street.

I briefly considered fleeing.

"John, welcome!" The host of the "Global" Blockchain "Summit" greeted me enthusiastically.

"Sandeep, hi." *Too late now.*

"So happy to see you!" He shook my hand vigorously. "Would you like a water?" He gestured to a large case of bottled water on the floor, its plastic wrapping mauled by thirsty bears.

"Fully hydrated, thanks."

"Great! You're up next. Our last few speakers canceled, so we're ready when you are."

A few minutes later I was plugged into the small TV monitor on the wall, giving the presentation to nine people that I had rehearsed for nine hundred.

Counting Your Chickens

My family owns a flock of chickens. Chickens, it turns out, lay eggs.

I know this sounds insane. You thought eggs were produced in a factory and packaged up in cardboard containers. But an animal makes them. It sits down on a nest and produces them out of some kind of egg hole. Nature—always something new!

It's pretty great to get fresh eggs, especially when you're friendly with the chickens that produced them. When you crack open a fresh egg, the yolk is electric yellow. Unlike the pale, watery yolks of store-bought eggs, those of fresh eggs are packed with an explosion of nutrients and goodness.

When we first got the chickens, I thought, *Free eggs!* Now I realize they're anything but free. They live in this postmodern coop that was designed by a team from London's Royal College of Art. They feast on high-end trail mix. They get electric heat in the winter. On a cost-per-egg basis, it's about a dollar each.

During the winter, chickens don't produce as many eggs. I'll go out to the coop and give them a pep talk. "Come on, chicks!"

I'll shout. (That's not sexist; that's reminding them where they came from.) "Let's get laying, ladies!"

"Daddy wants some breakfast!" I'll shout out the window a few hours later. "Lay 'em if you got 'em!"

Someone told me that egg production is related to the amount of daylight, so you can get them to produce more eggs during the winter by installing indoor lighting in your chicken coop. And I'm like, "Great. Now they want a tanning salon."

"Excuse me," a ponytailed gentleman in a large T-shirt interrupted. "I don't understand what this has to do with blockchain."

"Getting to it."

"Are we going to talk about how blockchain is transforming the **supply chain**?"

"No."

He stroked his beard excitedly. "What's interesting is that we'll be able to track chickens using **decentralized ledger technology**. Of course, the **consensus mechanisms** will need to be reworked to enable **trustless** transactions. Instead of **proof of stake**, we could have **proof of authority**, where . . ."

He went on like this for a full three minutes. I was irritated that I had been suckered into giving this talk, then sucker-punched by Comic Book Guy from *The Simpsons*. I did a quick temperature read of the audience, who were looking at me pleadingly.

"Why don't we hold questions to the end," I suggested, "or at least the middle?"

He folded his arms across his broad chest. "Very well."

Every couple of days, we'll go out to the coop and gather the eggs. We put them into this rectangular refrigerator container, where they go into the fridge in the garage, then eventually to the upstairs fridge when we're ready to eat them.

At twelve bucks a dozen, you want to be careful with these precious, freshest eggs. It's like they're filled with gold. So you can imagine my dismay when the container caught on the door of the garage fridge and *I dropped the eggs.* Yolks of sadness, a fluorescent yellow disaster, my own Chickenobyl.

"It's okay!" I shouted. "They're just a little dirty! We can still make an omelet!" I rushed to get some cardboard, scooping up the eggs from the floor of the garage.

It was horrifying, with sand and grit and engine oil all mixed in with the eggs. The chickens sometimes get in the garage, where they leave us gifts, so that was mixed in, too. It was a fully loaded floor omelet. A flomelet.

Every investing book tells you not to put all your eggs in one basket, because if you drop the basket, you lose all the eggs. That's true. But it's also true that you have to have *some* baskets. Otherwise you're shuttling eggs one at a time between the coop and the upstairs refrigerator.

Let's say that in 2015 you invested $10,000 into a classic portfolio of 50 percent stocks and 50 percent bonds. It was a great

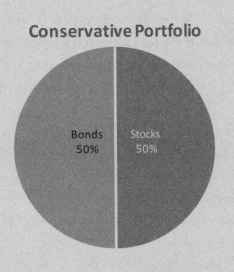

Conservative Portfolio

Bonds 50%

Stocks 50%

bull market, and you congratulated yourself three years later when your $10,000 had grown to $12,219: a 22 percent increase.

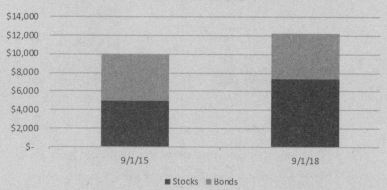

Now let's say you had further diversified that $10,000 into 65 percent stocks, 25 percent bonds, and 10 percent bitcoin. In other words, you put $9,000 into your "classic" mix and invested $1,000 in this new thing called bitcoin. Three years later your portfolio would have *quadrupled in value* to over $42,000.

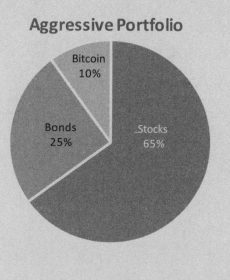

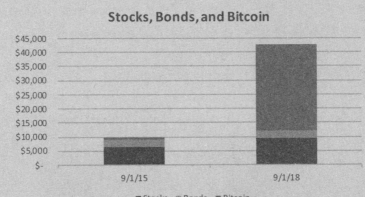

Stocks, Bonds, and Bitcoin

Now let's say that you had invested $9,000 in your "classic" mix of 65 percent stocks and 25 percent bonds, but the remaining $1,000 had been *diversified* into the top three altcoins: $500 into bitcoin, $250 into Ethereum, and $250 into Ripple. Three years later that $10,000 investment would be worth over $93,000.

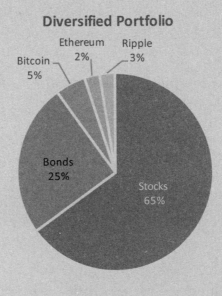

Diversified Portfolio

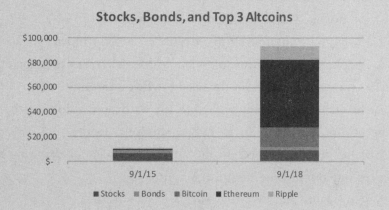

This is the chart that should give our financial planners a heart attack. What kind of investment increases by nine times in three years? And why did they not even know about it? Here's a chart showing the three strategies compared over that three-year time period.[59]

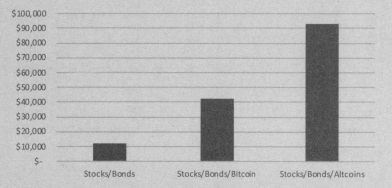

We diversify our stocks by buying a total stock market fund. We diversify our bonds by buying a total bond market fund. And we only put a maximum of 10 percent in diversified blockchain investments. We're trying to keep our eggs in lots of baskets so we don't end up with a flomelet.

"Excuse me, but I came to learn about blockchain," cut in Comic Book Guy. "This is the Global Blockchain Summit."

"Not global," I shot back, "and not a summit."

"What's more interesting for investors," he continued, "is how the **SHA-256 hash algorithm** stores data in **Merkle trees** to better enable trustless transactions without the need for **fiat currency** . . ."

As he went on, I calmly walked to the bathroom adjoining the conference room, leaving him to talk to himself. Really took my time. Washed my hands. Turned on the air dryer, which in that tiny space sounded like the turbine engine of a fighter jet.

When I came out, everyone was silent.

"As I was saying . . ." I continued.

To sum up:

+ Our first priority is to diversify our *overall* investment portfolio—to slice the pie into complementary pieces that balance each other out.

+ Our second priority is to diversify our *blockchain* investment portfolio as we have the time and interest.

This is how we put our eggs in the right amount of baskets. And that's no yolk.

"I appreciate the levity." He was the only one laughing. "That was good."

I decided to quit while I was ahead. "Thank you for your time," I said with a small bow.

Supply chain: the network of people that get stuff from suppliers to customers. Eggs go from poultry farms to distributors to warehouses to supermarkets to your belly.

Blockchain can simplify all this confusing paperwork, and let consumers see where their eggs are coming from.

Decentralized Ledger Technology: the Great Checkbook in the Sky.

Consensus mechanisms: Different blockchains have different ways of achieving consensus (i.e., agreeing on what's stored in the checkbook). You "earn" the right to vote when you contribute something to the network: either computing power (Proof of Work), money (Proof of Stake), or something else (Proof of Fill in the Blank). None of these systems are perfect.

Trustless: Blockchain geeks love to say "trustless," which is a confusing word. It means "letting you trust someone you don't know."

A better word is "trusted."

PLAIN ENGLISH
Ⓐ
Ⓑ Ⓒ

Hashing algorithm: scrambling data so that it cannot be read by someone else.

Cryptography, the technology at the heart of blockchain, uses hashing to protect sensitive data.

SHA-256: Short for "Secure Hashing Algorithm," it is a highly secure way of scrambling data.

Merkle trees: Named after computer scientist Ralph Merkle, it's an efficient way of looking up values in large data sets (for example, across an entire blockchain).

Fiat currency: dollars, pounds, Euros, etc.

Back in the lobby, a well-dressed gentleman was smiling at me from the couch. "That was rough," he laughed. "But entertaining."

"Agreed on both points." I shook my head, then shook his hand. "John Hargrave."

"I run a chain of coworking spaces in Boston," he went on, "and we're talking about starting a blockchain incubator. Would you be interested?"

"It depends," I answered warily. "Is your company called TechLab?"

"No way," he responded. "TechLab is the competition. We really want to build out Boston's blockchain community," he continued, then lowered his voice. "I'm confident we can do better than the Global Blockchain Summit."

"I've had bigger audiences in a confession booth," I joked.

"Oh, don't worry," he chuckled. "We're going to build some big audiences."

CHAPTER 36

The Blockchain Billionaires

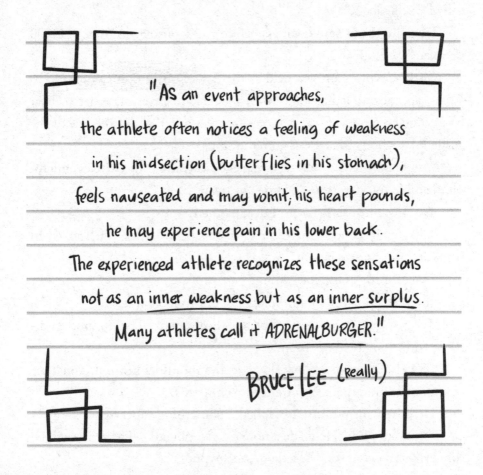

"As an event approaches,
the athlete often notices a feeling of weakness
in his midsection (butterflies in his stomach),
feels nauseated and may vomit; his heart pounds,
he may experience pain in his lower back.
The experienced athlete recognizes these sensations
not as an inner weakness but as an inner surplus.
Many athletes call it ADRENALBURGER."

BRUCE LEE (Really)

There's one secret to public speaking: Bomb a lot.

Bombing just comes with the territory. Even though your mind will torture you with the highlights reel for days afterward, the pain of your public embarrassment diminishes when you bomb again, setting off a fresh round of anguish.

After you bomb enough times, you come to a freeing realization: *you will survive.* I have bombed more than the German Luftwaffe and I'm still alive. Failure builds resilience. It gives you the courage to try new things. Bombing gives you a precious gift: what President Barack Obama called "fearlessness."[60]

That said, I was scared witless before going onstage in front of 2,500 people.

World Crypto Con was held at the Aria Convention Center in Las Vegas, an enormous hall filled with blockchain investors eager to hear how to make money. I was nervous—not so much about the size of the audience as about what I was going to say.

"You good?" asked the stage manager, threading the wireless microphone cable into my shirt. "Need some water?"

"No, I want to stay sharp," I deadpanned.

"Okay." He clipped the receiver to my belt. "Have you spoken in front of a Jumbotron before?"

"Once, at my cousin's wedding."

"It's distracting for a lot of folks. Try not to look at it."

"Try not to look at the Jumbotron," I repeated. "The Jumbotron directly within my field of vision."

"It's behind you. Just look down at the monitors in front. You'll see your presentation there. You want intro music?"

"Definitely intro music," I replied. "Something super high-energy."

"I'll tell the DJ." He made a note on a clipboard. "The lights will be very bright, so you won't be able to see anyone."

"Is there anything else?" I wondered. "Will I need to dodge falling bricks?"

"Not unless someone throws one at you," he deadpanned.

"Please welcome," shouted the emcee, "the author of the upcoming bestseller *Blockchain for Everyone*: JOHN HARGRAVE!"

Techno music blasting loudly. Colored spotlights dancing wildly. Crazy chaos, sound, and noise. Somewhere out there, girls and boys.

"How many of you want to become blockchain billionaires?" I shouted into the supernova. Applause.

"I've spent the past year studying these blockchain billionaires," I began, "and reverse engineering their secrets. There have generally been three roads to riches."

1. **They bought bitcoin early.** But they didn't just buy; they *believed*. Take the Winklevoss twins, who took the money they won from suing Mark Zuckerberg for stealing Facebook, then plowed it into bitcoin. But they didn't just buy; they held. Every time the market melted down, they held. They even had a mantra: "Spartans hold."

2. **They created blockchains of great value.** They weren't investors but inventors. Take Vitalik Buterin, the nineteen-year-old genius who saw that blockchain could be used not just for bitcoin but for decentralized applications (or **dapps**). He invented a platform for blockchain development—not to get rich, but to make something valu-

Dapps: short for "decentralized applications," the blockchain-powered apps that run on distributed networks of computers.

PLAIN ENGLISH
Ⓐ
ⒷⒸ

able. Investors made him rich anyway, pouring billions into Ethereum.

3. **They invested wisely in great blockchain projects.** Blockchain whales don't have to work anymore. What do they do? They reinvest that money into new blockchain projects. It's like building hotels on St. James Place in Monopoly, which generates revenue for you to reinvest in your Marvin Gardens hotels, and that lets you build hotels on Boardwalk. Game over.

DWeb: Short for "Decentralized Web," it means the entire ecosystem of dapps, just as "the Web" means the entire ecosystem of websites.

"Satoshi Nakamoto's vision was open-source money," I said, fishing a bill out of my pocket. "No longer would we need this stuff." I theatrically ripped up a dollar bill, and the crowd roared.

"But if it's open-source money, then why are we trying to hold on to it so much?" My eye caught the corner of the Jumbotron, and I was momentarily thrown. There was my head, blown up to the size of the convention center, mirroring my every move, but *with a half-second delay*. I quickly turned away.

"Let me tell you a true story," I continued. "There's a young man at my church who spent nearly a year doing humanitarian work in Africa, in one of the poorest countries in the world. He suffered through the most challenging living conditions: sleeping under a bed net with cockroaches scuttling all around him, trying to get enough nutrients in his diet, trying to help people meet their basic needs with no roads and no bridges to get it there.

"I saw him a few weeks ago. He was staying with his family, who have this beautiful home in Boston, and I said, 'What's it like going from *that* to *this*?' He got the far-off look in his eyes of someone who has seen a war." I paused.

"It was striking to see someone so young have that look of unspoken sadness and pain. He told me, 'Mostly it just makes me angry. Angry that we are so rich, and the rest of the world is so poor.'"

Now you could hear a ballpoint pen drop. "I admire billionaires like Bill Gates and Warren Buffett, who started the Giving Pledge to petition other billionaires to give away their wealth in order to improve the world." I grew heated. "*The new blockchain billionaires must follow suit.*"

Applause? No applause. Maybe I should rip up some more money.

"We are building the world we want to live in. The world I want to live in is one in which we're generating wealth not just for ourselves but for the world. Wealth for everyone, *not just the wealthy.*"

Smattering of clapping from the front. I clicked to a map of the globe, projected on the Jumbotron at near actual size.

"Picture the flow of money around the world like the flow of water. Countries with healthy financial systems have mighty rivers of money flowing between them: those are the thick lines. Countries with broken infrastructure, like Zimbabwe and Venezuela, have trickling creeks. Those are the thin lines."

"There are two billion unbanked people in the world today.[61] *Two billion!* If you're from a poor nation, and you move to the United States in search of a better life, how do you even send money to your family back home? It's slow, it's expensive, and the banks don't work. The system is broken."

A little more applause. Picking up steam. "Bitcoin and altcoins can unlock the flow of wealth and value like removing blockages in a stream.

But here's the truth, folks. Bitcoin is not free: there's a charge to send it. It's not scalable: it's getting slower as the blockchain gets bigger. And many people don't trust it.

"So my vision is even more radical than bitcoin. We need digital money that is four things.

+ **Free.** I'm not talking digital money with *low* fees: I'm talking *no* fees. When it comes to pricing, you can't beat free.

+ **Instant.** From wallet to wallet, anywhere in the world. The speed of money should be the speed of light.

+ **Scalable.** We need a digital currency that can power the entire human race. Trillions of transactions each day.

+ **Trusted.** All money systems come down to trust. In everything we do, in everything we say, we must work to build that trust. That is my charge to you.

"Free, instant, scalable, and trusted. FIST." I clicked to my final slide: a raised fist, done in the Soviet propaganda style.

"If you're with me"—I raised my voice—"then raise your FIST. This is how we lift the world out of poverty." Was anyone raising their fist? I was staring into a nuclear furnace.

"I'm John Hargrave, and I wish you health, wealth, and happiness." I bowed but was unable to hear the level of applause over the deafening techno music and blinding lights.

———

Behind the curtain, the stage manager was busy fishing the microphone out of my shirt. I desperately wanted to ask him how it went, but I had learned that stage managers were busy managing the stage. He probably hadn't heard a word I said.

"Hey." A voice called in my direction, and I turned around. It was Charlie Shrem, one of the legends in the bitcoin community. He was dressed in a T-shirt, a sport coat, and a hat, surrounded by his entourage: the very picture of a bitcoin mogul.

He looked me up and down. "What's your name again?"

CHAPTER 37

Crypto Bros vs. Blockchain Pros

"I think the blockchain world is splitting into two groups," I began. It was only a few hours after my keynote speech, and I was leading a private training session with a couple of partners from Rosewind Capital, a new blockchain hedge fund. The conference room at the Aria was standing room only.

"The first group is out to get rich quick. They're speculators. They try to time the market. They 'pump and dump.' I call these guys—and they're practically all guys—the *crypto bros*.

"The second group is out to get rich slowly. They're investors with impact. They look for blockchain projects with real value. They hold for the long term. I call these folks the *blockchain pros*.

"Crypto bros versus blockchain pros. Also the title of a terrible rap album." A few chuckles. "Now, today you had the choice of two activities: you could come to our private session, or you could go where?"

"Poker tournament," offered one of the gentlemen at the front table.

"You could go to a *poker tournament*. You could come here and learn about investing, or you could gamble. And you made the right choice. I applaud you." Once I started applauding, everyone else followed.

"Poker is a game of skill," called out a voice from the back of the room. I searched out the voice, which was coming from a guy wearing a white linen shirt and aviator sunglasses.

"Hey, take off the sunglasses so I can see you."

"It's bright in here, man." He bared his teeth. "I'm near the window."

"You say poker is a game of skill," I repeated.

"If you're good, it is."

"And what do you do for a living?"

"Crypto trader."

"Right, but what do you do to make *money*?" A few people laughed.

"Crypto trader, full-time."

"And you make money?"

"Lots."

"Well, check back with us in a year. And five years. And ten years. Because eventually you're going to take a big bath. Meanwhile, the rest of us will be enjoying a leisurely soak. Soaking up the growth."

"When Lambo?" asked a young bearded guy from the same table, and a number of people laughed.

"If you're just joining us," I explained, "'When Lambo' is slang for 'When will I get my Lamborghini,' an overpriced car with terrible gas

> *If you look at historical data, there is a striking resemblance in the price movements and volatility during the early days of NASDAQ and bitcoin. Each new asset class involves a process of price discovery and market validation which takes place over a period of time. Meanwhile, the traditional wisdom works: diversify your portfolio and hedge against risk.*[62]
> —Navroop Sahdev, Head of Economic Strategy, 55Foundry

mileage: 10 city/17 highway."[63] I had been waiting all day to use this one. It's the small pleasures.

"I've given up on getting rich quick," I went on. "Too much risk. In my quest for a billion-dollar company, I put my entire company into blockchain. I paid dearly for that decision. But our losses have learnings. When you suffer setbacks—and you will—can you see them as tuition paid to the school of life?

"I learned so many valuable lessons. I learned my own strength. I learned my own voice. I learned to do my own laundry."

A few chuckles.

"Great risk can result in great reward. But great risk can also result in great regret." I smiled. "When it comes to blockchain, *never invest more than you can afford to lose*. One hundred percent. High-risk gambling, day trading, speculating—that's the way of the crypto bros."

From the back of the room, I saw the table of guys get up and walk out the side door. "For most of us," I continued, "it's better to build wealth slowly. I did hedge my risk in one way: I didn't touch my personal investments. So now I'll open my kimono and show you my personal portfolio."

Value Investing on the Blockchain

The basic principles of value investing are simple; we've updated them for the age of blockchain.

+ Adopt a long-term "value investing" strategy, looking for great companies offered at a fair price.

+ Use steady-drip investing, auto-withdrawing the same amount every month into your portfolio.

+ Keep the majority of your portfolio in stocks and bonds.

- ✦ Consider blockchain your "alternative investments," a small slice of the pie.

- ✦ To find promising blockchain investments, do your homework (qualitative and quantitative).

- ✦ Your blockchain investments can be a mix of bitcoin, altcoins, and traditional public companies.

Let's look at my personal portfolio to see how you might put this into action.

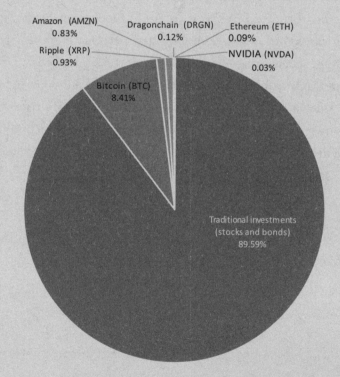

Amazon (AMZN)
0.83%

Dragonchain (DRGN)
0.12%

Ethereum (ETH)
0.09%

Ripple (XRP)
0.93%

NVIDIA (NVDA)
0.03%

Bitcoin (BTC)
8.41%

Traditional investments
(stocks and bonds)
89.59%

Traditional investments make up about 90 percent of my holdings: stocks, bonds, and real estate. The simplest way is just to buy a total stock market fund and a total bond market fund. (See **Reference Guide 3** for sample percentages for each.)

Bitcoin (BTC) makes up the biggest piece of my blockchain investment (about 8 percent), because I've done my homework and determined that, for me, bitcoin seems to have the best stability and long-term future of all the blockchain investments—not to mention the most brand awareness.

Altcoins like **Ripple (XRP)**, **Ether (ETH)**, and **Dragonchain (DRGN)** make up around 1 percent, because my research suggests they represent the blockchain platforms of the future.

Traditional companies like **Amazon (AMZN)** and **Nvidia (NVDA)** round out my investments, because my analysis indicates they're great companies that are positioned to profit from blockchain.

Transparency is important to me. I want you to know my investments so you can see where I might be biased. I don't share this with you so that you'll invest in the same things: in fact, I hope you don't. I would rather you do your own research, draw your own conclusions, and make your own decisions.

The goal of all this is to learn together. I hope that we all make the boldest, best-informed decisions that we can, sharing both our successes and our failures. Open-source data: that's the spirit of blockchain.

"Rather than making yourself rich, your investments allow you to make a rich life," I pointed out.

I paused, feeling unexpectedly emotional. "You know, I've spent the past year rebooting my thinking, rebooting my business, rebooting my life. It was hard, really hard." I swallowed. "But I'm so glad I did it. Otherwise I wouldn't be here with you today.

"We need a reboot now and again. Otherwise we get buggy and slow. Blockchain technology is rebooting our government, our financial systems, our health care systems, our distribution of wealth, and a million other things. That needs to happen from time to time. Now's the time.

"I have this little Moleskine notebook . . . I'm not getting paid by Moleskine, by the way, I just think it's a funny name, like they're covered in little mole pelts: Canadian mole trappers, the mole fur trade, moles on the verge of extinction, Moles Are Beautiful movement, MAB mobs, mole protection legislation, mole sanctuaries, leading to mole overpopulation, then mole bounty hunters and more Moleskine notebooks."

I opened a page. "That's just an idea I wrote down here." Some people were laughing; some were staring at me, wondering when I was going to talk about bitcoin.

"Anyway, I write down little affirmations in my Moleskine notebook in the Bruce Lee style, and here's the latest."

I am living my highest good
I am living my highest good
I am living my highest good
I am living my highest good
I am living my highest good
I am living my highest good

I am living my highest good

I am living my highest good

I am living my highest good

I am living my highest good

I am living my highest good

I am living my highest good

I am living my highest good

I am living my highest good

I am living my highest good

"My highest good, at least for now, is to make blockchain interesting and fun. To explain it in plain English. To get the other 99 percent of the world investing—in a safe and sensible way—so that this ecosystem will grow. To guide its growth and development in a way that's good for the world."

I smiled and held up three fingers. "Easy to understand, easy to use, easy to invest. But I can't do it alone. I hope you'll join me. I hope everyone will join me. I hope we can bring . . ."

I clicked to a slide of my book jacket, the book you're reading now, and led the room in saying:

". . . blockchain for everyone!"

CHAPTER 38

Leaving the Lambo Show

> " Experience shows that an athlete
> who forces himself to the limit
> can keep going as long as necessary.
> No condition is too 'tough' to take in order to win.
> Such an attitude can be developed only if winning
> is closely tied to the practitioner's ideals and dreams. "
>
> BRUCE LEE

It was a glorious October day in Las Vegas, and I squinted happily as I carried my luggage to the curb outside the Aria hotel. The porter came along behind me, wheeling our trade show display.

I looked in my wallet, and found I had only $2 in cash. "I'm sorry, my friend," I said, smiling, and handed it to the bellhop. "It's all I've got."

He accepted it graciously. "No problem."

I called an Uber, then I called my wife.

"Hey, babe," she answered. "How was the show?"

"I think we got some business."

"That's great news," she said.

"More great news: I got a check. My first paid speaking gig."

"Woo-hoo!" she said, doing her best Homer Simpson impression. "Here's some more great news: as of this month, we are officially back in the black."

I flashed to an image of Atlas carrying the world on his back before finally setting it down on a luggage cart. "What a relief," I sighed.

"It gets better," she said. "I have even more great news."

"Even more?" I asked. "Raisin toast is free now?"

"I heard back on my application."

"And?"

"They accepted me!" she exclaimed.

"Congratulations!" I felt a heady mix of emotions at this news. I had to sit down on my suitcase.

"That's not all. They awarded me a *full scholarship*!"

"Holy Lord."

"I am so excited!" she said, and I could feel her vibrating.

"The Boston University School of Theology. BUST! You're going to a seminary named after cleavage."

"You know, Martin Luther King went there."

"They put the 'Dr.' in Dr. Martin Luther King, Jr."

"I've got it all figured out," she went on. "I'll still work for Media Shower full-time and do my degree part-time. I've got my first semester all drafted up already." She paused. "You're okay with this, aren't you?"

"I am so thrilled for you," I told her. It was another beginning, and another end.

"Are you sure?"

"You have supported me in everything I've ever done. When things got as dark as they could get, you never gave up. You are a saint. It makes sense, and it's my turn. Absolutely."

"It'll take a few years. I don't even know what I want to do with it."

"I think you should become a preacher."

"No," she said. "Really?"

"Then I can tell people, 'You know, I'm not a preacher, but I *have* slept with one.'"

"This is amazing!" she said giddily.

"I'm so proud of you." I looked up. "Hey, I'll call you from the airport. Uber's here."

Riding with Strangers

Your entire life, people have been telling you that you should never accept rides from strangers. Then came Uber.

Now we not only hop into a stranger's used Prius, we actually pay for the privilege. That's because the experience is so much better than the alternative: hailing a taxi.

Do you remember riding in taxis? You got in this humid plexiglass box that smelled of coconut air freshener. The seat was missing springs. A TV screen blared noise at you. You watched the meter tick upward, like a time bomb in reverse, worrying that the driver was deliberately taking you the long way.

Then you were supposed to tip! Are you tipping the driver for *not killing you*?

Uber solved all those problems in one neat stroke. Flat fares. Normal cars. Transparent routes. Despite Uber's many shortcomings, it has driven a stake through the black heart of the taxi industry. Uber has made the world better by making the whole experience better.

The taxi industry was ripe for disruption. You could not reform the taxi industry from the inside: the bad behaviors, the suffocating regulation, the hostility between drivers and customers . . . They were all too deeply ingrained.

The taxi industry couldn't just graft technology onto their old business model: Uber destroyed the old business model. Economists call this **creative destruction**,[64] and today we see old (centralized) companies struggling to integrate this new (decentralized) blockchain technology before they, too, are destroyed creatively.

Creative destruction: when an old industry or institution is destroyed by a newer, better alternative (think taxis versus Uber).

KEY TERM

Uber is not a blockchain. While Uber is in some ways decentralized, it's highly centralized in others. Who owns the pool of drivers? Uber. Who owns the user-generated ratings? Uber. Who owns all that valuable customer data? *Uber über alles.*

The next wave of creative destruction will be on Uber itself. Imagine Unber: a decentralized version of Uber, run on blockchain-based smart contracts. When you want a ride, you pull up the Unber app, punch in the destination, then send the estimated payment (in bitcoin) to a smart contract.

I pick you up in my used Prius, drive you there, making small talk and offering you a bottle of sparkling water (we're on our best behavior). Once we arrive, the smart contract sees from our GPS coordinates that the ride has been completed, and releases the payment to the driver. We rate each other five stars.

In this system, no one "owns" the data, the payment, or the ratings: it's all recorded on a public blockchain, a public ledger, the Great Checkbook in the Sky. Drivers get a bigger cut of the earnings, because there's no uberhead.

Creative destruction is everywhere. It can result in revolution, but it can also result in evolution. If we're flexible and open-minded, if we welcome change and embrace growth, we can emerge better and stronger. If not, well, you can always drive the world's last cab.

"Going to the airport?" my Uber driver asked, helping me load all my gear into the back of his SUV.

"Going home," I said. "Finally."

"You in town for the auto show?"

"No, a blockchain convention."

"Blockchain." He closed the hatchback. "What's blockchain?"

"It's a long story." I climbed into the back seat.

"Check that out," said my Uber driver, fastening his seat belt. "A

Lamborghini." He grunted. "And a Bugatti. A Ferrari. That's a . . . let's see, that's a McLaren. And . . ." He whistled. "That is a Lykan Hyper-sport."

I had been standing next to a luxury auto display, right in the middle of the Aria drop-off circle. I hadn't even noticed. "So they just park these things here?" I asked.

He laughed. "There's a big auto show in town this week. Must be one of their events. Man, check that out." He pulled closer to the Hyper-sport, craning to see. "That's a $3 million car. Look, it has diamonds embedded in the headlights. Check out the crowd. No one even cares about these other cars."

I went back to my phone. "You check them out," I said. "I'm check-ing in. To my flight."

"You will probably never see another one of those again," he said, slowly pulling his gaze away.

"Well," I said, putting down my phone, "who knows what the future holds?"

The Blockchain Investor Portfolio
A Step-by-Step Template for Investing in Digital Assets

Set aside a monthly amount to put into your investments—even if it's just $100. Ideally this will be an automatic withdrawal from your bank account into your portfolio, so you can "set it and forget it."

Allocate your monthly investment into three slices: stocks, bonds, and blockchain (between 2 and 10 percent).

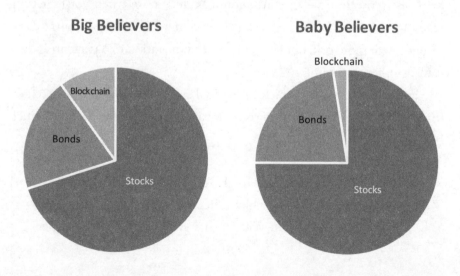

For example, let's say you decide on a steady-drip investment of $500 per month. Each month, you split up that $500 and invest it according to your risk tolerance and belief in blockchain:

+ Big believer: 70 percent traditional stocks, 20 percent traditional bonds, 10 percent blockchain

+ Baby believer: 75 percent traditional stocks, 22.5 percent traditional bonds, 2.5 percent blockchain

Big blockchain believers are comfortable with more risk (i.e., losing money) for the potential of more reward (i.e., making money). Their monthly drip payment of $500 would go $350 into stocks, $100 into bonds, and $50 into blockchain investments.

Baby believers want to invest some money in blockchain—but not enough to break the bank if this turns out to be a really weird dream. Their monthly drip payment of $500 would go $375 into stocks, $113 into bonds, and $12 into blockchain.

As a rule of thumb, your percentage of bonds can roughly equal your age. Bonds provide protection when the stock market goes down: you need less protection when you're younger, and more when you're getting ready to retire. You can keep a larger percentage in stocks if you're comfortable with more risk, but try not to exceed the ratio of 75 percent/25 percent in either direction.

Rather than trying to pick individual stocks, bonds, and blockchain investments, the simplest way to invest is through **index funds**, which buy the entire market for you:

+ **Stocks.** U.S. investors might consider the Vanguard Total Stock Market Index, which offers broad diversification with low fees. It has a ten-year annual average return of 7.4 percent. You can purchase it through online brokerages like TD Ameritrade (www.tdameritrade.com).

✦ **Bonds.** For exposure to the entire bond market, consider the Vanguard Total Bond Index, with low fees, purchased through the same online brokerage. As stock prices go down, bond prices generally go up, so bonds act as a counterweight to help protect your investment.

✦ **Blockchain.** No blockchain market index fund exists at the time of this writing, so the simplest solution is to buy bitcoin each month through an online exchange like Coinbase (coinbase.com). You can diversify through buying additional tokens, which we'll cover next.

Thus, the "big believer" with a monthly investment of $500 would invest:

✦ $350 in her total stock market fund, through her online brokerage;

✦ $100 in her total bond market fund, through her online brokerage;

✦ $50 in bitcoin, through her online bitcoin exchange.

Rebalance the ratios every six months. Make a recurring appointment on your calendar for January 1 and July 1. This means you may need to sell your bitcoin and reinvest those gains into traditional stocks and bonds, or vice versa.

While this is not easy to do when the blockchain market is soaring, it provides protection when the blockchain market is souring. Consider the investors who rode the blockchain boom of 2017, only to lose it all in 2018. Those who converted their blockchain profits back into stocks and bonds (i.e., rebalanced their portfolios semiannually) protected their newfound wealth.

Using this approach, you'll have a research-proven method for investing in the total stock and bond markets while keeping a slice of the pie for blockchain investments. You'll be able to enjoy the upside of blockchain investments while still being protected if things go south.

But beyond bitcoin, how do you pick those investments? Until we have an easy-to-use blockchain index fund, you can find new blockchain opportunities using **qualitative analysis** (research and judgment) and **quantitative analysis** (research and numbers), covered in the next two guides.

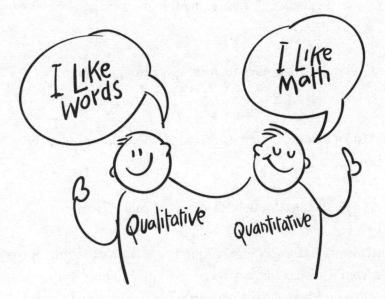

Successful investors use both qualitative and quantitative analysis. They're the conjoined twins of investing.

It would be foolish to buy an altcoin entirely on your Investor Score-card rating in **Reference Guide 2** without digging into the underlying numbers. Similarly, it would be foolish to make investment decisions purely on the charts in **Reference Guide 3** without doing the Investor Scorecard.

If you're better at one than the other, then partner up with someone who complements you. Use each other as a sounding board, and try to find the truth together. Open-source data—that's the spirit of block-chain.

The Blockchain Investor Scorecard

Using the Blockchain Investor Scorecard, you can decide whether a blockchain token or altcoin is a sound investment. This is called "due diligence," also known as "doing your homework." You'll come out of this exercise more informed than the vast majority of blockchain investors.

ᗷ BITCOIN MARKET JOURNAL   THE BLOCKCHAIN INVESTOR SCORECARD

At *Bitcoin Market Journal*, our analysts use this "scorecard" to evaluate new blockchain projects and tokens. By rigorously asking the same questions across several different categories, the blockchain investor or entrepreneur can have an "apples to apples" comparison of different business ideas.

For each question in the list, assign a score from 1 (lower potential) to 5 (higher potential). The score for each question is averaged at the end of each section, and the score for each section is averaged at the end.

	Higher potential (5)	Lower potential (1)	Value
MARKET			
Problem that it solves *Is there a clear problem solved by this token?*	Identified	Unfocused	
Customers *Can you clearly identify who will use this token (job title, demographics, etc.)?*	Reachable and receptive	Unreachable or unlikely to adopt	
Value creation *If a user adopts this token, how much value will be added to his/her business or lifestyle?*	High and identified	None	
Market structure *What is the composition of the market this token will serve?*	Emerging or fragmented	Concentrated or mature	
Market size *Is the potential market too small, too large, or just right?*	$100 million+	<$10 million	
Regulatory risks *How likely are further regulations on this market, and tokens in general?*	Low	High or highly regulated	
AVERAGE MARKET SCORE *Average the six scores above*			
COMPETITIVE ADVANTAGE			
Technology/blockchain platform *Is the token built on a well-known standard blockchain, or is it built from scratch?*	Existing blockchain	New blockchain	
Lead time advantage *Does the team have a head start on companies working on a similar idea?*	Strong	None	
Contacts and networks *What is the team's ability to access key players in this market?*	Well-developed	Limited	
AVERAGE COMPETITIVE ADVANTAGE SCORE *Average the three scores above*			

Bitcoin Market Journal nor its parent company, Media Shower Inc., PROVIDE FINANCIAL, ACCOUNTING, INVESTMENT, TAX, LEGAL OR OTHER SERVICES AND in no event shall its Website, the Services or any Content be deemed financial, accounting, INVESTMENT, tax or legal advice. NEITHER USE OF THE WEBSITE or content NOR THE PROVISION OF SERVICES creates, nor IS IT INTENDED TO create, ANY PROFESSIONAL RELATIONSHIP BETWEEN THE COMPANY AND ANY USER OF THE WEBSITE OR THE SERVICES, AND IS NOT PROTECTED BY THE ATTORNEY-CLIENT OR OTHER PRIVILEGE. YOUR USE OF THE WEBSITE, content AND SERVICES IS AT YOUR OWN RISK.

BITCOIN MARKET JOURNAL   THE BLOCKCHAIN INVESTOR SCORECARD

	Higher potential (5)	Lower potential (1)	Value
MANAGEMENT TEAM			
Entrepreneurial team *Does the team have a demonstrated track record of success?*	All-star "supergroup"	Weak team or solopreneur	
Industry/technical experience *Does the team have "10,000 hours" of experience in this industry?*	Super track record	Newbies	
Integrity *Does the team demonstrate scrupulous honesty and complete transparency?*	Highest standards	Questionable	
AVERAGE MANAGEMENT SCORE *Average the two scores above*			
TOKEN MECHANICS			
Token required *Does the problem truly require a token, or is it a "bolt-on blockchain"?*	Impossible without	Token unnecessary	
Value added *Does the token add a new type of value, or is it "another one of those"?*	Highly differentiated	Copycat token	
Decentralized *Is it truly decentralized (like a mesh network), or is it run by the company (like a cell tower)?*	Users do the work	Company does the work	
Token supply *Is there a known quantity of tokens, or can more be issued in the future, diluting the value?*	Fixed, predictable	Uncertain, inflatable	
Public exchange *On which digital exchanges will the token be listed?*	Known, reputable	Unknown or disreputable	
MVP *Is there an existing product, or a Minimum Viable Product?*	Functioning product	White paper only	
AVERAGE TOKEN SCORE *Average the six scores above*			
USER ADOPTION			
Technical difficulty *Will a nontechnical person be able to understand this idea?*	Nontechnical	Highly technical	
Halo Effect *Is the token strongly associated with well-regarded brands or institutions?*	Strong halo effect	Weak or no halo	
Buzz *Are people talking about it? How many followers do they have on social media?*	High social buzz	Low social buzz	

BITCOIN MARKET JOURNAL   THE BLOCKCHAIN INVESTOR SCORECARD

	Higher potential (5)	Lower potential (1)	Value
OVERALL SCORE *Weighted average of the five section scores above*			

For blockchain investors, the Scorecard should be viewed as a tool for identifying promising opportunities. For tokens that score highly, the investor will want to do a deeper competitive analysis.

For blockchain companies, the Scorecard can be used as a tool for strengthening the idea. Better still, a company like Media Shower (www.mediashower.com) can be hired to fill it out more objectively. For more information, see our peer-reviewed paper: https://ssrn.com/abstract=3146191 and our YouTube instructional video: https://youtu.be/NkCMVyf8OOI .

Be ruthless in your analysis. Your default answer should be "I'll pass," saying no to many opportunities before you say yes to one. When you do say yes, you can invest with confidence—because of all the research and analysis you've done using our scorecard.

Metrics for Blockchain Investors

Blockchains have network effects: the more people who use a blockchain, the more valuable it becomes.

Like a telephone network, as a blockchain attracts more users, it becomes more useful to all users. The more users, the more connections, the more value. Assuming a fixed number of tokens, each token becomes more valuable, because it's "holding" more value in the network.

Total Network Value

To see how this theory holds up in real life, let's compare blockchain investors versus the overall blockchain market capitalization (i.e., the total value of all altcoins) through the end of 2016, and see if it follows a similar pattern.

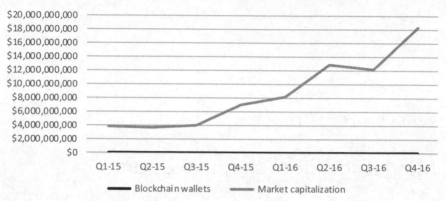

In plain English, as the number of blockchain users (measured by wallets) increased linearly, the overall value of the blockchain market increased quadratically. The rocket took a while but finally achieved liftoff. So far, so good. Then came 2017.

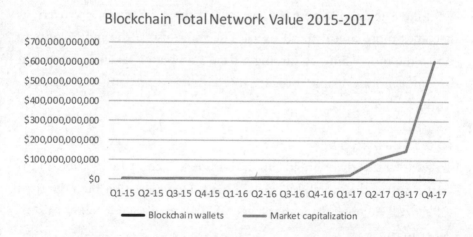

Blockchain mania hit a fervor in December 2017, driving the value of bitcoin and altcoins to dizzying heights. Let's see what happened after that:

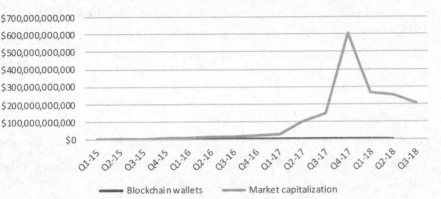

Blockchain Total Network Value 2015-2018

Blockchain users continued to grow at a steady clip (about two million per quarter), but the market cap was all over the market map.

The blockchain investor can use Total Network Value as "guardrails" for a market that's overpriced or underpriced. The Rocket Rule can be simply charted using basic tools like Microsoft Excel, where I will now right-click and add a "polynomial trend line":

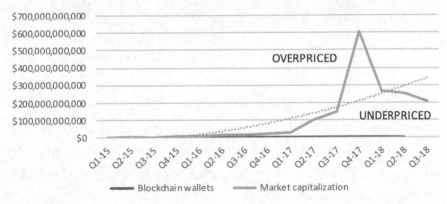

Blockchain Total Network Value 2015-2018

The dotted line shows the trend, suggesting that the fourth quarter of 2017 would have been a good time to sell blockchain investments, and the second quarter of 2018 would have been a good time to buy. Which is what I personally believe: for me, this passes the common sense test.

To sum up, you can chart the Total Network Value of an altcoin for any period of time—let's say monthly—using any online blockchain exchange. Then you can chart the "Rocket Rule," or quadratic growth formula, using a "polynomial trend line" in Microsoft Excel. This can signal for tokens that are on sale.

Value Per User

Another way that analysts value network companies like Facebook and Twitter is by looking at Value Per User. We divide their market capitalization by their number of monthly active users.

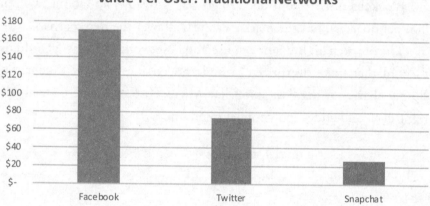

Value Per User: Traditional Networks

Data as of 11/20/18. Sources: Omnicore Group, Yahoo Finance.

Of the top social media networks, the Value Per User generally ranges from $25 to $250. These values fluctuate, but they give us some guardrails. With blockchain assets like bitcoin, we can take market cap (total bitcoin x price per bitcoin), then divide by number of monthly active users. It looks like this:

Value Per User: Blockchain Networks

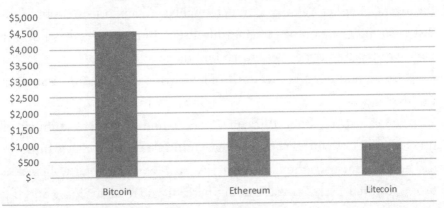

Data as of 11/20/18. Sources: Bitinfocharts, CoinMarketCap.

Of the blockchains we can track, the Value Per User range is between $1,000 and $5,000 per user. We would expect it to be higher than for social media networks, since these users are much more valuable: they're not just mindless ad-consuming machines, as on Facebook. They're actively trading value.

Here's the best part: blockchain Value Per User, despite the market turmoil, has stayed relatively consistent. Take a look at the mania of November 2017 versus the depression of November 2018:

Value Per User: Guardrails

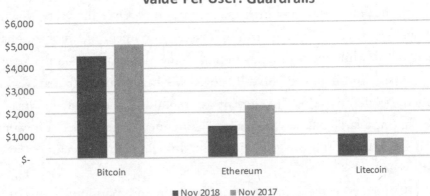

In plain English: more people were actively using bitcoin in 2017, so the overall market value was much higher. When prices dropped in 2018, so did the number of monthly users, but the overall Value Per User has stayed in the $4,500 to $5,000 range.

This is good news. It means there is a rhyme and a reason, a method to the madness.

One caveat: It's often difficult to determine the precise number of users on a blockchain. (People can have multiple wallets.) So we must do the best we can with the data we have—such as using total wallets as a proxy for total users, as we're doing here. If you're analyzing a specific altcoin, you might also use *number of transactions* as a proxy for total number of users. Not perfect, but it's what we have.

Here again, we see the Value Per User in 2017 was likely overpriced, and the value at other times was likely underpriced. If you have done the qualitative analysis on an altcoin using the Blockchain Investor Score-card and you like what you see, then consider buying when the Value Per User dips below the dotted line.

Increase in Connections

You may know about Tony Hsieh, the brilliant and eccentric founder of the online shoe retailer Zappos.

One of Hsieh's pet projects has been to remake the downtown Las Vegas area into a thriving high-tech community. Over the years, downtown Vegas—the "waving cowboy" Vegas you see in old movies—has stagnated, while the big money moved to the glitzy casinos on the Strip.

Hsieh (pronounced "Shay") moved his headquarters to Las Vegas, then began attracting investment to rebuild the downtown area—including a large public space called "Container Park," built out of shipping containers and overseen by a flamethrowing praying mantis. (Hey, it's Vegas.)

Container Park is an interesting experiment. Boutique shops and eclectic restaurants surround a large playground that's enjoyed by both

kids and adults. In one corner is a large stage for regular nighttime per-
formances, complete with sofas and lounge chairs. It's a hangout spot, a
meeting place, and a shopping mall all rolled into one.

Fittingly for an Internet entrepreneur, Hsieh has come up with a
number of quantitative metrics for judging the success of his high-tech
community. One of these is the number of "collisions," or serendipitous
encounters, between strangers.

To technology innovators like Tony Hsieh, Steve Jobs, and Marissa
Mayer, innovation happens when people from different backgrounds
"collide" with each other in unexpected ways. Hsieh even measures
"return on collisions," or the value of his investment as measured by the
number of random encounters.

This idea of "people colliding" (in a good way) also applies to blockchain technology. You've seen it throughout this book, with our blockchain incubator, investor meetups, and blockchain conventions. A third
metric, Increase in Connections, captures the spirit of Hsieh's "return on
collisions."

Remember the Rocket Rule: as the number of users grows linearly,
the number of connections grows quadratically. If we know the number of
users, we can calculate how many connections are added in each time
period. (Think how many more connections are added to Hsieh's park as
he attracts more people.)

To find the number of connections c, we use the formula

$$c = \frac{n(n-1)}{2}$$

where n is the number of users.

Thus, if Hsieh has 50 people wandering around Container Park, the
number of possible connections is $\frac{50(50-1)}{2}$, or 1,225 possible collisions.
Double the number of people (to one hundred), and we *quadruple* the
number of possible connections (to 4,950).

Just as the value of Hsieh's downtown Las Vegas project grows quadratically as it adds more people, so do the value of blockchains grow as we add more people.

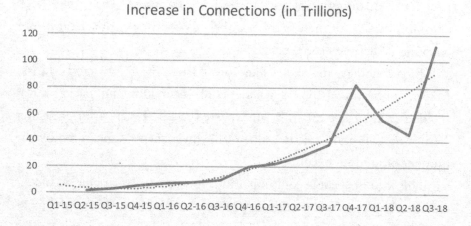

Increase in Connections (in Trillions)

This shows the number of connections of the overall blockchain market as measured by the number of blockchain wallets. As we discussed above, the dotted trend line (which you can easily chart in Microsoft Excel) provides "guardrails" to indicate whether the market might be overpriced or underpriced.

Through the third quarter of 2017, the blockchain market was priced according to what we'd expect. (The solid line matches the dotted line.) As the market went manic at the end of 2017, investors rushed to open up new blockchain wallets (overpriced), then fell into a depression (underpriced).

The takeaway: the blockchain is about people. The number of users on a blockchain matters, because that increases connections, and connections increase value. That applies to downtown Las Vegas, as well as the blockchain investing market.

AFTERWORD

In the interest of writing a strangely addictive story that you would want to read cover to cover, I occasionally combined events, changed names or identifying details, simplified dialogue, or created composite characters. Always I tried to stay true to the spirit of the story.

These names I made up for illustrative purposes, and they do not describe or endorse any real blockchain project: SolarCoin/SolarChain, DriveCoin/DriveChain, RewardCoin/RewardChain, PowerUpCoin/PowerUpChain, ContentCoin/ContentChain, IdentityCoin/IdentityChain, TrustCoin/TrustChain, and the Global Blockchain Summit.

If you enjoyed this book, please sign up for our free newsletter at www.bitcoinmarketjournal.com.

ACKNOWLEDGMENTS

Blockchain is decentralized, and so was the creation of this book. Profound thanks to my wife, best friend, and partner, Jade Hargrave. Thanks to the rest of my family: Isaac Hargrave, Luke Hargrave, John Hargrave, Pat Hargrave, Patrick Hargrave, Keri Hargrave, Donna York, and Terry York.

Thank you to my loyal agent, Cathy Hemming, and my incredible editor, Jeremie Ruby-Strauss, whose suggestions improved this book immensely. Thanks to the phenomenal team at Gallery Books: Aimée Bell, Jen Bergstrom, Allison Greene, Mackenzie Hickey, Anabel Jimenez, Brita Lundberg, Jen Long, Sydney Morris, Monica Oluwek, Caroline Pallotta, Jennifer Robinson, Nancy Tonik, Diana Velasquez, Jennifer Weidman, and Abby Zidle.

Thanks to the terrific team at Media Shower, especially Pete Angus, Wendy Grieco, Mary Hiers, Kevin Kelly, Rob Montepeluso, Jessica Ridella, Cliff Robinson, Lisa Strickland, and Jess Ullrich. Thanks to Joe Caruso for guiding us, Richard Kastelein for advising us, and Peter Relan for believing in us.

Thanks to my Game Night friends: Kirk Worcester, Ben Laubach, and especially Evan Karnoupakis for many helpful discussions about blockchain.

Thanks to Emre Tekisalp and Sid Coelho-Prabhu from Coinbase, and Greg DiPrisco from MakerDAO. Thanks to Matthew Mottola, Bruce Bracken, Liane Scult, and Paul Estes from Microsoft. Thanks to Adam Williams and Eric Spire of World Crypto Con. Thanks to Ryan Colby and Brinkley Warren of Token Fest.

Thanks to Rob Nance of CityBlock Capital for the idea of investor certification, and to Miko Matsumura for the idea of open-source data. Thanks to Hanaan Rosenthal and Dr. Travis Winden of Rosewind Capital for letting me tap into their infinite knowledge about blockchain trading. Thanks to Peter Pavlina of Hamersley Partners for many valuable discussions about how to make blockchain investing accessible to everyone. Thanks to Daivi Rodima-Taylor for the discussion about Zimbabwe, and Ligda and Carl Massicotte for that about Venczuela.

Thanks to the Boston Blockchain Association, especially Peter Brooks, Mac Cameron, Denise de Murcie, Ryan Fox, Dominic Grew, Gregory Hassett, Frank Makrides, Henry Moodie, Shamir Ozery, Eric Roux, and Mark Schinkel. Thank you to Blockchain Shark Tank: Mac Cameron, Andrew Flessa, Dianne Mueller, Jessica Ridella, Navroop Sahdev, Jay Stevens, and Jodi Heights.

Thank you to all the blockchain experts who sat for interviews, including Shada AlSalamah, Dan Birman, John Clippinger, Olga Feldmeier, Dan Kinsley, Josh Lawler, Hunter Mefford, Ofer Lidsky, Nick Powley, Nimit Sawhney, Navroop Sahdev, and Dr. Tal Sines.

Thanks to Genevieve Martineau, Ned Rhinelander, and Chris Scott for the dot-com memories. Thanks to Ken Accardi for giving a theme to the book, and Heather Kelly for helping me save the cat. Thanks to all my test readers, especially Stephen Leahy, Amy Harris, and Jim Merullo.

Thanks to the amazing Adrian Medel Aceiro for making my illustrations look great. Thanks to Babson College for the Moleskine notebook. And thanks to the Boston Chinese Investment Club for the pen.

Finally, a huge thanks to our terrific community of one hundred thousand blockchain investors—and growing!

NOTES

Chapter 3: The Epic Origin Story

1. Let's agree that the plural of "bitcoin" should be "bitcoin," not "bitcoins." And no capital *B*.

Chapter 4: The Accountant Monk

2. Casey, Michael J., and Paul Vigna. "In Blockchain We Trust." *MIT Technology Review*, May 18, 2018, www.technologyreview.com /s/610781/in-blockchain-we-trust/.

3. Avakian, Talia. "The 10 Strangest Things That Have Been Used as Money Around the World." April 19, 2016, http://www.business insider.com/alternative-forms-of-currency-2016-4.

Chapter 5: It's Raining Money

4. Poole, Robert Michael. "The Tiny Island with Human-Sized Money." May 3, 2018, http://www.bbc.com/travel/story/20180502-the-tiny -island-with-human-sized-money.

5. Vazquez, Laurie. "How Ramen Noodles Became King of Prison Currencies." August 23, 2016, https://bigthink.com/laurie-vazquez /how-ramen-noodles-beat-cigarettes-to-become-a-prison-currency.

Chapter 6: Act Like You Belong

6. "National Bank Note." Wikipedia, January 21, 2018, en.wikipedia .org/wiki/National_Bank_Note.

7. "ICOs Have Raised Billions—But Now VCs Are Swooping In." *CB Insights Research*, June 12, 2018, www.cbinsights.com/research /blockchain-ico-equity-financing-vc-investments.

8. McLeay, Michael, et al. "Money in the Modern Economy: An Introduction." Bank of England, March 14, 2014, www.bankof england.co.uk/quarterly-bulletin/2014/q1/money-in-the-modern -economy-an-introduction.

9. "Ripple (Payment Protocol)." Wikipedia, October 6, 2018, en.wikipedia.org/wiki/Ripple.

10. "Bitcoin Cash." Wikipedia, September 12, 2018, en.wikipedia.org /wiki/Bitcoin_Cash.

11. "EOS.IO." Wikipedia, October 16, 2018, en.wikipedia.org/wiki /EOS.IO.

12. "Stellar (Payment Network)." Wikipedia, October 18, 2018, en.wikipedia.org/wiki/Stellar.

13. "Litecoin." Wikipedia, October 4, 2018, en.wikipedia.org/wiki /Litecoin.

14. For the full video of Burniske's presentation, see https://youtu.be /ooKXtFoMjtY. Also see Burniske, Chris, and Jack Tatar. *Crypto-assets: The Innovative Investor's Guide to Bitcoin and Beyond.* McGraw-Hill Education, 2017.

Chapter 7: The New New York Stock Exchange

15. "Dutch East India Company." Wikipedia, December 24, 2018, en.wikipedia.org/wiki/Dutch_East_India_Company.

Chapter 12: Canadian Yoda

16. Konrad, Alex. "How Lightspeed VC Jeremy Liew Looks for the Next Bonobos and Snapchat." *Forbes*, July 1, 2015, www.forbes .com/sites/alexkonrad/2015/05/05/how-lightspeed-vc-jeremy -liew-looks-for-the-next-bonobos-and-snapchat/#1aef435261d9.

17. Balakrishnan, Anita. "Snap Closes up 44% After Rollicking IPO." CNBC, March 7, 2017, www.cnbc.com/2017/03/02/snapchat -snap-open-trading-price-stock-ipo-first-day.html.

18. Huston, Caitlin. "Snapchat Founders, Investors Cash Out Nearly $1 Billion in Snap IPO." *MarketWatch*, March 3, 2017, www .marketwatch.com/story/snapchat-founders-and-investors-sell -millions-of-shares-in-snap-ipo-2017-03-01.

19. Constine, Josh. "Why Snapchat Spectacles Failed." *TechCrunch*, October 28, 2017, https://techcrunch.com/2017/10/28/why-snapchat -spectacles-failed/.

20. Mukherjee, Supantha. "App Redesign Haunts Snap as Investors Flee." Thomson Reuters, May 2, 2018, www.reuters.com/article /us-snap-results-stocks/app-redesign-haunts-snap-as-investors-flee -idUSKBN1I31QD.

21. "Initial Public Offerings: Eligibility to Get Shares at Broker-Dealers." U.S. Securities and Exchange Commission, September 6, 2011, www.sec.gov/fast-answers/answersipoelightm.html.

Chapter 13: For the People, by the People

22. Anderson, Christa M., et al. "Forest Offsets Partner Climate-Change Mitigation with Conservation." *Frontiers in Ecology and the Environment*, Wiley-Blackwell, August 14, 2017, https://esajournals .onlinelibrary.wiley.com/doi/full/10.1002/fee.1515.

23. Lee, Sherman. "Bitcoin's Energy Consumption Can Power an Entire Country—but EOS Is Trying to Fix That." *Forbes*, April 19, 2018, www.forbes.com/sites/shermanlee/2018/04/19/bitcoins-energy

-consumption-can-power-an-entire-country-but-eos-is-trying-to-fix
-that/#67695ed31bc8.

Chapter 14: Investing vs. Speculating

24.   Furman, Phyllis. "Investment Banker Hopes to Issue More Rock 'n' Roll Bonds." Knight Ridder/Tribune Business News, October 26, 1998.

25.   Boulden, Jim. "David Bowie Made Financial History with Music Bond." CNNMoney, January 11, 2016, https://money.cnn.com /2016/01/11/media/bowie-bonds-royalties/.

26.   Christman, Ed. "The Whole Story Behind David Bowie's $55 Million Wall Street Trailblaze." *Billboard*, January 14, 2016, https://www .billboard.com/articles/business/6843009/david-bowies-bowie-bonds -55-million-wall-street-prudential.

27.   Chen, James. "Bowie Bond." Investopedia, March 7, 2018, www .investopedia.com/terms/b/bowie-bond.asp.

Chapter 15: The Comedy Economist

28.   See the full John Oliver segment at https://youtu.be/g6iDZspbRMg.

29.   "Why Does the Federal Reserve Aim for 2 Percent Inflation over Time?" *Frequently Asked Questions*, Board of Governors of the Federal Reserve System, January 26, 2015, www.federalreserve.gov /faqs/economy_14400.htm.

30.   Hanke, Steven H. "The Troubled Currencies Project." Cato Institute, September 30, 2018, www.cato.org/research/troubled-currencies.

Chapter 16: The Blockchain Investor Scoreboard

31.   I am grateful to the legendary Babson College entrepreneurship professors Jeffrey Timmons, Stephen Spinelli, and Andrew Zacharakis for the "Timmons Model of Entrepreneurship," which is the framework used for our Blockchain Investor Scorecard. Zacharakis, Andrew, et al.

"Appendix 1: Quick Screen Exercise." *Business Plans That Work: A Guide for Small Business.* New York: McGraw-Hill, 2004.

32. Adest, Abbi. "Rupert Murdoch Comments on Fox Interactive's Growth." Seeking Alpha, August 9, 2006, https://seekingalpha.com /article/15237-rupert-murdoch-comments-on-fox-interactives-growth.

33. Barnett, Emma. "MySpace Loses 10 Million Users in a Month." *Telegraph*, March 24, 2011, www.telegraph.co.uk/technology/myspace /8404510/MySpace-loses-10-million-users-in-a-month.html.

34. Kahneman, Daniel. *Thinking, Fast and Slow.* New York: Farrar, Straus and Giroux, 2015.

35. Feynman, Richard P. "Cargo Cult Science." Caltech Commencement Address, 1974.

Chapter 18: Unreserved

36. Buffett's actual quote is "It takes twenty years to build a reputation and five minutes to ruin it. If you think about that you'll do things differently." At least, that's the quote attributed to him in countless online articles; I was unable to find a source.

37. Harari, Yuval Noah. *Sapiens: A Brief History of Humankind.* New York: Harper, 2015, p. 180.

Chapter 21: Moody McMarketson

38. "The Four-Way Test." Guiding Principles, Rotary International, January 13, 2019, https://my.rotary.org/en/guiding-principles.

Chapter 22: We the People

39. Wright, Emma. "Founder's Spotlight: Nimit Sawhney of Voatz." CIC, January 14, 2018, https://cic.com/podcasts/founders-spotlight /voatz.

40. Ross, Aaron. "Protest, Tear Gas in Congo as Sassou Nguesso Seeks

to Extend Rule." Reuters, March 20, 2016, www.reuters.com
/article/us-congo-election-idUSKCN0WM0B2.

41. "Venezuelan Constituent Assembly Election, 2017." Wikipedia,
August 2, 2018, https://en.wikipedia.org/wiki2017/Venezuelan
_Constituent_Assembly_election.

Chapter 24: The Gold Rush

42. I am grateful to H. W. Brands for his excellent book, from which
many of this chapter's anecdotes are taken. Brands, H. W. *The Age
of Gold: The California Gold Rush and the New American Dream*.
London: Folio Society, 2015.

43. Marshall, James W. "James W. Marshall's Account of the First
Discovery of the Gold." The California Gold Country, www
.malakoff.com/marshall.htm.

44. Lee, Alex. "Blockchain Patent Filings Dominated by Financial
Services Industry." PatentVue, Envision IP, January 12, 2018, www
.patentvue.com/2018/01/12/blockchain-patent-filings-dominated
-by-financial-services-industry/.

45. Huillet, Marie. "Wells Fargo Files Patent for Tokenization System
to Protect Sensitive Data." Cointelegraph, July 18, 2018, https://
cointelegraph.com/news/wells-fargo-files-patent-for-tokenization
-system-to-protect-sensitive-data.

Chapter 26: The Bubble Bursts

46. Manjoo, Farhad. "How to Survive the Next Era of Tech (Slow
Down and Be Mindful)." *New York Times*, November 28, 2018.

47. Szabo, Nick. "Micropayments and Mental Transaction Costs."
Satoshi Nakamoto Institute, https://nakamotoinstitute.org/static
/docs/micropayments-and-mental-transaction-costs.pdf.

48. This idea is similar to the Basic Attention Token (basicattentiontoken

.org), except that BAT still relies on users watching ads, which is a model that's doomed to fail.

Chapter 27: Private Parts

49. Graham, p. 131.
50. Personal interview, July 19, 2018.
51. Riley, Michael, et al. "The Equifax Hack Has the Hallmarks of State-Sponsored Pros." Bloomberg, September 29, 2017, www .bloomberg.com/news/features/2017-09-29/the-equifax-hack-has -all-the-hallmarks-of-state-sponsored-pros.

Chapter 28: Glass and the Abyss

52. Lacy, Sarah. "Elon Musk on the Best Way to Eat Glass." TechCrunch, https://techcrunch.com/2010/08/05/elon-musk-on-the-best-way-to -eat-glass-video/.

Chapter 31: Ending the Beginning

53. Thanks to my friend Joe Peacock for inspiring the yuan pun.
54. As an agricultural product that has to be harvested, dried, and sold, it is difficult to estimate exactly how much "all the tea in China" would be worth, but estimates place any given day's supply at between $2 billion and $4 billion. With a net worth of $36 billion, Jack Ma should be able to cover it. Sources: "How Much Tea Is There in China? And How Much Is It Worth?" *Quora*, January 28, 2015, https://www.quora.com/How-much-tea-is-there-in-China -And-how-much-is-it-worth; and "Jack Ma." *Forbes*, October 15, 2018, www.forbes.com/profile/jack-ma/.
55. Febvre, Lucien, and Henri-Jean Martin. *The Coming of the Book: The Impact of Printing 1450–1800*. New York: Verso, 1976.

Chapter 32: Tearing It Up

56. Zhang, Xing-Zhou, et al. "Tencent and Facebook Data Validate Metcalfe's Law." *Journal of Computer Science and Technology* 30, no. 2 (2015), pp. 246–51, doi:10.1007/s11390-015-1518-1.

57. Hundt, Reed. Wall Street Journal Business and Technology Conference. September 18, 1996.

58. 2016 Survey of Consumer Finances (SCF). Board of Governors of the Federal Reserve System, August 9, 2018, www.federalreserve .gov/econres/scfindex.htm.

Chapter 35: Chicken Fight

59. All data taken from CoinMarketCap.com as of September 1, 2018.

60. "President Barack Obama." *WTF with Marc Maron Podcast*, June 22, 2015, www.wtfpod.com/podcast/episodes/episode_613_-_presi dent_barack_obama.

61. Demirgüç-Kunt, Asli, et al. "The Global Findex Database 2017." World Bank, 2018, https://globalfindex.worldbank.org/.

Chapter 37: Crypto Bros vs. Blockchain Pros

62. Personal interview, September 3, 2018.

63. "Fuel Economy of 2018 Lamborghini Vehicles." U.S. Department of Energy, October 15, 2018, www.fueleconomy.gov/feg/bymake /Lamborghini2018.shtml.

Chapter 38: Leaving the Lambo Show

64. Schumpeter, Joseph A. *Capitalism, Socialism, and Democracy.* Virginia: Wilder Publications, 2018.